The Gift of Values II

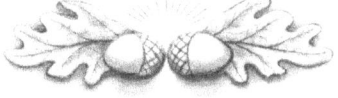

A Resource for Family Devotions

Rosie Boom

Great Oaks from Little Acorns

The Gift of Values - Volume Two.
Copyright © 2008 Rosie Boom

Published by Boom Tree Publishing
549 Kara Rd, R.D. 9 Whangarei 0179, New Zealand
Website: www.rosieboom.com

Rosie Boom contact details:
Email: rosie@rosieboom.com
Rosie's Blog: www.rosieboom.com
Website: www.rosieboom.com

All rights reserved. No part of this book may be reproduced or transmitted in any form or by any means, electronic or mechanical, without prior written permission.

All scripture quotations, unless otherwise indicated, are taken from the HOLY BIBLE, NEW INTERNATIONAL VERSION®. NIV®. Copyright © 1973, 1978, 1984 by International Bible Society. Used by permission of Zondervan. All rights reserved. The Scripture quotations taken from the New American Standard Bible are copyright © 1960, 1962, 1963, 1968, 1971, 1972, 1973, 1975, 1977, 1995 by The Lockman Foundation. Used by permission. www.Lockman.org

Every reasonable effort has been made to trace owners of copyright material in this book, but in some instances this has proved impossible. The publisher will be glad to receive information leading to more complete acknowledgements in subsequent printings of the book, and in the meantime extends apologies for any omissions.

Cover Design by Stephen Cooling
Printed and bound by Lightning Source

National Library of Australia Cataloguing-in-Publication

Boom, Rosie, 1956-
The Gift of Values. A Devotional Resource for Families.

1st ed.
ISBN 978-1-921161-16-2 (v. 2)

1. Family 2. Moral education. 3. Christian Life. 4. Values clarification. I. Title

248.845

2nd ed.
ISBN 978-0-9951123-5-3

I dedicate this book to my parents,
Evan and Leone Harris.
They have been my lifelong inspiration
and daily example of each
and every value in this book.
I love you Mum and Dad.

"Thank you so much for sharing your thoughts and wisdom in your book, The Gift of Values. I have been struggling with our morning devotions - trying to inspire our six children, who are all different ages, and trying to keep them all interested. Your book really has been an answer to prayer. I feel like God has touched my heart and kissed my forehead."
Joanne Van Vliet, New Zealand

"Well done for writing such a readable, entertaining, honest and challenging book!"
Barbara Jones, New Zealand

"Some would say values are better caught than taught. But both approaches are needed. It respects a child's intellect to explain clearly what generosity is, for instance, and why we should be generous. The Gift of Values is an excellent tool for teaching values. Use it while you also demonstrate consistency in living out those values before your children, and you will effectively pass on Godly values to the next generation."
Dave & Neta Jackson, authors of the *Trailblazer Books* and *Hero Tales*, America

"Family devotions should be an exciting time, a time that everyone looks forward to with great anticipation. This book, The Gift of Values will help create such an atmosphere. It's a fantastic book filled with inspiring stories, quotes, and wisdom, with lots of practical ideas. It is the best resource for family devotions that I have ever read. I only wish that I had had something similar when my children were growing up as I am sure I would have used it again and again over the years."
Don James, Senior Pastor, Crossroads Community Church, New Zealand

"We recently were sent a copy of your book, The Gift of Values - Volume One. What a tremendous blessing it has been to me. I was so encouraged to read about your Milly. I have taken on the fact that I am training a champion! It came in perfect time, when I was feeling like I had failed as a mum. I am hoping you will write another book!"

Alex and Lisa Snary, Mongolia.

"This book should not be in everyone's bookcase, it should be on the coffee table where it can be easily accessed every day. Jesus tells us in Matthew 28:19-20 to go into all the world and teach all nations to observe the things which He has commanded us. Rosie is doing just that by compiling a book full of the values that Jesus himself taught while He was on earth, and that the Holy Spirit continues to teach us through God's Word. This book gives us, in a format that any parent can easily use, the resources and experiences that Rosie and Chris have had in the raising of their children. It goes on the highly commended list."

Rob and Sharon Holding, Radio Rhema, New Zealand

"I received your book The Gift of Values about a week ago. We love it! I love the fact that you have stories to relate to along with quotes and other applicable ideas. It is exactly how we teach our children. Thank you for heeding God's call to write this book. May it bless many other families as it is blessing ours!"

Marla, New Zealand

"I just bought a copy of The Gift of Values ~ Volume One and sat down today and read it right through. We had our 'Bible Time' a bit late this afternoon and I read my boys the first story. They really loved it, and I could tell they got the message intended! Thanks for following your inspiration to write these books."

Lisa Crosse, New Zealand

S. D. G.

The Gift of Values II ~ Tabs

Value One GENEROSITY 9

Value Two ENCOURAGEMENT 47

Value Three SELF CONTROL 79

Value Four COMPASSION 107

Value Five PATIENCE...137

Value Six FORGIVENESS 161

The Shema

Hear O Israel; the Lord our God, the Lord is one. Love the Lord your God with all your heart and with all your soul and with all your strength. These commandments that I give you today are to be upon your hearts. Impress them on your children. Talk about them when you sit at home and when you walk along the road, when you lie down and when you get up. Tie them as symbols on your hands and bind them on your foreheads. Write them on the doorframes of your house and on your gates.

Deuteronomy 6:4-9

The Gift of Values II

Contents

Preface 1

How to use this book 3

Value One GENEROSITY 9

    The All for God Club 11

    The Silver Thread 24

    The Box 35

Value Two ENCOURAGEMENT 47

    The Castle of Giant Despair 49

    The Two Frogs 60

    In the Camp of Death 67

Value Three SELF CONTROL 79

    Waldo Pigginson 81

    The Two Pirates 90

    The Boy with Gifted Hands 97

Value Four COMPASSION 107

    Ninepence.. 109

    William and the Ring 120

    The Watchmakers of Haarlem 128

Value Five PATIENCE 137

    Hannah and the Corn 140

    Uncle Hendrik's Moustache 148

    Show Me How to Live 154

Value Six FORGIVENESS 161

    Hard Choices 163

    The Shepherd's Call... 175

    The Color of Spring 185

Epilogue... 193

Acknowledgements.. 194

More from the Boom family album... 195

About the Author... 197

Preface

I have had the great joy of writing Volume Two of *The Gift of Values* in our new, temporary home - a somewhat run-down, ninety-year-old barn in Whangarei, New Zealand. Earlier this year, Chris and I bought eleven acres of farm land, complete with river and majestic native trees.

As soon as school is over for the day, the children roam all over the land, canoe down the river, make tree huts and teepees, ride their pony and go exploring. It's an adventure wonderland for our six children!

Chris and I have enjoyed doing up the barn - concreting floors, putting in windows and installing a cast iron wood-burning stove. I love it here. Truth is, I could stay here forever, but Chris and Josiah and I will soon begin building the new Boom family home. I know, however, that none of us will ever forget the wonderful memories we are making here in our 'pioneering' days. And for me, it has been a fantastic place to write this book - rich in experiences and anecdotes and learning.

Not long after we first moved into the barn, a fierce storm swept in. In fact, it was to be the first of *two* 'hundred year' storms to hit the area in a matter of a couple of months. Chris and Josiah hurried to brace the east end of the barn, which was waving in and out under the battering of the gale force winds. They worked for hours outside in the torrential rain, securing the roof which was threatening to lift off, rescuing stock as the river rose higher and higher, and battening down sheds and equipment. The girls and I worked feverishly inside the barn, moving furniture into the middle of the room and lifting the carpet away from the corners where the rain was driving in. The power went off for three days. We had two sleepless nights as we listened to the wind rage against us, wondering if at any moment the roof would disappear. The barn creaked and groaned, but stood strong.

When the storm abated, we ventured out to inspect the damage. Lying all over the countryside were big trees, uprooted by the winds. I stared in astonishment at some of these massive trees - at their beautiful foliage, impressive trunks, and then in surprise at their roots. Nearly all of the fallen trees had very shallow root systems. It was a profound picture to me of the importance of the values we are trying to teach our children. I long for each of my children to send down deep, strong roots, which will help them stand in the storms of life.

As I stood looking at the fallen trees, I imagined the root of honesty reaching deep into the soil; the roots of compassion and perseverance holding the earth, and the root of courage nurturing the tree that grows above. I understood all the more that these values are vital to our children's futures. For storms will surely come to all of us.

So much of the real 'work' of parenting involves the hidden places of the heart. We can't see the roots that are growing deep and strong in our children's lives. At times we catch glimpses of progress and growth, and we rejoice. But unfortunately it is all too easy to become focused on the outward appearances - the trunk, the branches, the leaves. The storm forcefully reminded me that a tree is only as strong as its roots. It's not what's visible on the top that counts. It's the strength and depth of what lies below.

My prayer is that this book will help you remember the importance of those things that are hidden deep - the inner integrity and character that will be the making of your children. I pray you'll be inspired to teach these values to them, no matter how small the beginning seems. Oak trees do not grow overnight. But they do grow from little acorns!

How to use this book

Perhaps some of you reading this book have already worked your way through *Volume One*. If so, you will be familiar with the way the book is laid out, and will probably have worked out the best way to use it in your family times. For those of you who haven't read *Volume One*, I have included the How to Use this Book section again in this volume. It gives you a brief outline of the structure of the book and a few suggestions on how you may use it with your children. Of course, there is no 'right way' - you need to find what works for you and your children.

My prayer is that it will help you instil in your children a love for God, a thirst for truth, and give them a solid foundation of true values.

We all long to see our children develop a strong character - a character which will help them navigate their way through this ungodly world, not just by the skin of their teeth, but as shining examples to others.

We have the awesome responsibility of planting the seed of God's word in the hearts of our children. Within the seed of strong, clear moral values lies the fruit of joy and personal fulfillment. Our children will lead happier and more fulfilling lives if they have a strong foundation of Christian values.

It is never too early (or too late) to start. Some of you reading this may be thinking, "How can I possibly teach my children the values of honesty and forgiveness when my own life has been such a mess? Aren't I being hypocritical trying to teach my children something that I am still struggling with myself?"

Absolutely not! You can teach your children not only from the things you've done well, but also from the things that you wished you'd done differently. Richard Eyre writes in his book *Teaching Your Children Values*, "We all want to teach better than we ourselves have learned. We all want our children to surpass us." Amen to that!

I have written this book with my own family in mind, aware that many of you also have families with a fairly big spread of ages. Ideally, we want to make devotions a time which all the children enjoy. This can be a challenge, but I believe it can be done. I have included stories that will appeal to the younger ones, and that the older ones can listen in to as well. Always be thinking of age-appropriate questions that you can ask each of the children. I have included thought provoking quotes for the older children. In our own family, I have generally stayed with one value for at least a fortnight. That way, the children become aware of it in their own lives, and begin to look for examples of it in the books they read and in everyday life. My suggestion would be to read the first story, and ask questions on the first day. Over the next few days, you could look at the Bible references and discuss some of the quotes. Enjoy plenty of discussion times. Choose further readings from the suggested reading list. There are plenty of ideas for further developments if you so choose. I hope it's all here for you - a small bite if that's all you have time for, or a three course meal if you're hungry!

Each chapter includes the following...

A brief introduction

At the beginning of each new value, I have written a short introduction for parents to read. It will give you a brief overview of what the chapter will contain, and some thoughts written especially for you, the parent.

Stories

The words 'Once upon a time' never fail to thrill me. A story can move you; challenge you; open your eyes. There is nothing like a good story to get a truth across. Jesus knew that. He was a master storyteller.

In each chapter I have included stories that you can share with your children, and suggestions for further reading as well. But don't forget - your own life is a book full of wonderful stories you can share with your children. You may never become a children's writer, but you can learn to tell your own stories. Your children will love to hear you share about your own life. As you read a new chapter, ask God to remind you of any thing in your life that will help apply the truth. It may be just a small incident that happened when you were a child, but as you share it, it will have real impact. And once you start looking for these 'stories', you'll find them everywhere.

Encourage your children to tell their own stories as well. You'll be amazed how even the youngest can tell something so pertinent to the value that you're talking about. It only takes one of them to say, "I remember when…" and the others will be bursting to have their say.

Think about it

Jesus asked a lot of questions. He wanted people to search out truth for themselves. Get into the habit of asking lots of questions in your devotional time. Get your children thinking. Once you develop the habit, you'll find it becomes very easy to think of thought provoking questions, even while you're reading a story. I have included some prompts to get the ball rolling.

Something to do

Over the years, I've tried to think of practical, creative ways I can illustrate a truth that we've been learning about in our devotional times. I'll share some of these in each chapter, and they'll probably be the only prompt you need to think of plenty of your own. Van Dyke once said, *"Opportunities swarm around us, thicker than gnats at sundown. Every day we walk through a swarm of them."* Creative ideas are like that. Once you train your eyes to see them, they come thick and fast. But you have to be looking for them.

And if you feel you haven't got a creative bone in your body - don't worry! Creative ideas are given by God to be shared. Borrow the ideas of others and make them your own. There are plenty enough ideas to go around!

So said...

A few carefully crafted words can hold so much truth and meaning. They offer great starting points for lively discussion. The quotes I list in each chapter are just the tip of a huge iceberg.

A caution here. If your older children plan to search the internet for more quotes, proceed carefully! The internet is a mine field, and quotes can be a storehouse for offensive material. I always type *'Inspirational quotes on...'* in the search engine, and have not read an offensive one yet. However, the one time I left the word *'inspirational'* out, I was bombarded with some really dubious quotes.

I have found some great quotes on blackboards outside shops, in the newspaper and in books. Go hunting yourself and pin them up in different places around your house. A notice board in the 'little room' is a great place for displaying your finds!

Words to live by

There are countless scriptures that apply to each topic, but I have listed just a few as a starting point. If you have older children, encourage them to use these as a springboard for their own Bible studies.

Boom clip

In this book, I have shared with you many personal experiences and anecdotes that have happened in the Boom household. We are a very normal family, and have had plenty of 'learning' moments - squabbles, fights, disagreements, dramas etc. But we have also had a rich, endless supply of joy and laughter!

How to use this Book

Dig deeper

As much as possible, get your children to do some research on the topic. A simple idea is to get one of them to look up the particular word in the dictionary. Just discussing some of the listed meanings will offer a goldmine.

There are many different ways you can develop the basic ideas in this book. There are countless movies that illustrate the different truths and an endless supply of books and biographies you can enjoy. At the end of each chapter I have listed books or DVDs which we as a family have enjoyed, that have helped reinforce the appropriate truth.

However, I must say it's a real challenge to find movies that are totally free of content that may offend. A great resource we have used is Focus on the Family's entertainment review site, *www.pluggedinonline.com*. Here you can get a detailed review of a big selection of movies and videos from a Christian perspective. It lists each occurrence of bad language, violence or sexual content, and gives a good overview of the movie's plot. If you want to enjoy a relaxed movie evening with the family, without feeling on edge and wondering what's going to come on the screen next, check it out on this site first.

I encourage you to check for yourself the ones I have listed in the Dig Deeper section before you view them.

☙

One Last Word

Recently I read a great pithy saying. "Think it, ink it." In other words, write things down! We forget so easily - even things we're sure we'll never forget! Get into the habit of writing things down. Aside from helping you to remember, it serves to solidify and clarify what you've learnt. It also ensures that later you can go back and "Do it, review it!" (As the second half of the saying goes.)

I hope that as you work through this book, you will encourage your children to do lots of 'inking!' When each of my children turned four years old, I gave them a big, blank book. It is *the* place to write down scriptures that they're memorizing, great quotes, poems - anything that is inspiring and worth remembering. The children do art work in there as well. It was one of the best things I ever did. I encourage you to do the same. Make sure you get a well bound book with good quality art paper - you want it to last. This will be a book each child treasures as they grow older. They aren't expensive, but even if they were, they'd be worth every cent!

As your children learn about the values covered by this book and try to put them into practice, watch them carefully - not so much for what they do wrong, but for what they do right. Look for every opportunity you can to praise them. Reinforce and acknowledge their attempts to be kind or honest. For example, Samuel has just this minute run in to tell me that Jacob has fallen off the tramp and hurt himself. I praise him for being kind and caring, and his face glows.

Praise your children for every little step they take in the right direction, and give plenty of encouragement along the way. The Duke of Wellington was asked near the end of his life what one thing he would change if he could live his life over again. "I would give more praise," he replied.

May God bless you as you embark on this wonderful journey.

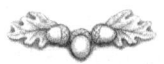

Value One

GENEROSITY

I recently asked a teenager what she'd like to do after graduating from school. I was surprised when she gave the same answer several other teenagers have also given me. "I'm going to be a millionaire." Oh, I see.

When I was growing up, the usual answer was a nurse, a teacher, a secretary, a doctor. I don't think I ever heard someone say they were going to be a millionaire - times have changed. But the really interesting thing is, each of the young people I spoke to, plan to reach their millionaire status without 'working'.

In today's world, young people are much more aware of all the possibilities open to them. Books like *Rich Dad, Poor Dad* and *Smart Kid, Rich Kid* by Robert Kiyosaki present a different path to financial freedom and are full of helpful ideas. Kiyosaki also talks a lot about generosity.

Generosity is a fundamental part of the Christian faith. John 3:16 tells us, "For God so loved the world, that He *gave* His only begotten Son, that whoever believes in Him should not perish, but have eternal life."

Jesus went on to tell His disciples, "Freely you have received, freely give." *(Matthew 10:8 NIV)*

Our attitude to money will have enormous repercussions in our lives. Now, I must hasten to add that I don't have a problem at all with the idea of being rich. In fact, there have been many times I've wished I were. Recently, I read about the time someone asked Thomas Edison, the great inventor,

The Gift of Values

what his goal in life was. Quick as a flash, Edison replied, "To make money." Then he immediately added, "So I can keep inventing." When I read that, I knew exactly what Edison meant! Money can be a huge blessing in our lives, and can make it possible for us to achieve the dreams and the callings God has placed in our hearts. But the *love* of money is a curse. Timothy encourages us to be content with food and covering, and then warns, "Those who want to get rich fall into temptation and a snare and many foolish and harmful desires which plunge men into ruin and destruction. For the love of money is a root of all sorts of evil, and some by longing for it have wandered away from the faith, and pierced themselves with many a pang." *(1 Timothy 6: 8-10 NASB)*

God has called us to serve others, and that will involve work. I for one don't want my children to fall into the lifestyle of the 'idle rich'. I hope and pray they'll know how to work hard, and live their lives to help and serve others.

Our children are growing up in a world of huge possibilities, as well as one that is riddled with hedonism, greed and insatiable desire for riches. We are going to have to teach them what 'the true riches' are. We need to help them discover the wonderful truth of Jesus' words - "It is more blessed to give than to receive." *(Acts 20:35 NASB)*

And we must prayerfully do our very best to raise children who value generosity above wealth.

‌ ◌ß

The All for God Club

"Mum!" My heart was pounding as I ran up the drive. My cheeks felt hot. "Mum! Look!" I waved the letter as I ran.

Mum looked at me with a puzzled expression while I tried to catch my breath. "It's a letter… addressed to me…" I panted. "The secretary of *The All for God Club*!"

Last year my sister, Emily and I started a club with our two friends, Marilie and Aletia. It's called The *All for God Club*. Our motto is 'To live our lives all for God, and serve Him by helping others.'

"Go on," urged Mum.

I took a deep breath and started to read.

"Dear Miss Boom, (I had a giggle at that.)

We are a God-fearing trust and have at our disposal a sum of money, that we wish to give to a worthy cause. It has come to our attention that your club is in the business of identifying such worthy causes and providing them with funding to carry out God's purposes.

We entrust you with this money to use wisely for the cause of your choice, as you feel led by the Holy Spirit. God bless you as you give your all for Him."

I grinned at Mum. "It's from Uncle Jonny and Auntie Donna! And look!" My hands were shaking as I took a cheque out of the envelope and waved it in front of Mum's face. "$500! Can you believe it?" I did a little jig on the front porch.

Mum took the letter and read it again, and laughed out loud. "That's fantastic, Eliza! God saw what you did for us last year, and now He's multiplied back to you the money you gave."

You see, earlier this year, my mum and older brother and sister were going on a missions trip to the Yasawa Islands near Fiji. Our club wanted to help them raise the money they needed. Over the next few months, we did a concert, a puppet show, lots of odd jobs, and ran two 'cafes'.

The Gift of Values

For the cafes we did lots of baking and then invited people around the neighborhood to come for lunch or afternoon tea. We raised $120 for the trip. "It's so cool!" I said. "I'm going to ring the other girls straight away!"

Marilie's squeal was so loud I had to hold the phone away from my ear. The next day we had a club meeting and started talking about how we could use the money.

"I think we should send some money for blankets for the people in Pakistan," said Aletia. "So many have lost their homes in the earthquake, and winter's coming."

So we sent $100 to World Vision for some blankets. You know, when I licked the envelope and put it in the letterbox, I felt so warm inside! I know that the blankets will warm lots of children over there in Pakistan.

Do you know what we did next? We bought a pig for a family in Cambodia! The pig only cost us $45, and it will mean that the Cambodian family will be able to earn some money and send their children to school.

Then we bought a goat for a family in Afghanistan! With Tear Fund's plan, each family that receives a goat promises to give away the first kid the goat has to some other poor family. That means the blessing just keeps being passed on.

A couple of weeks later, our Christian radio station here in New Zealand started a special outreach for the orphans in Fiji. They asked people to fill shoeboxes with gifts and a Bible, and send them to the radio station. They would then send them on to Fiji.

As soon as we heard about it, we knew we wanted to help. So *The All for God Club* went shopping the next day. We had so much fun choosing all sorts of stuff to put in our shoeboxes - teddy bears, clothes, sweets, hair ties and of course, a Bible. I decorated my box with shiny paper and stickers.

The exciting thing is that since then, other people have heard about our club and have given us money. So we have more money to give away!

The other day we saw a video about the Ruel Foundation; an organization that goes into remote villages in Asia and finds children that have terrible deformities, like cleft palates and facial tumors. Their parents can't afford to pay for an operation to make them better, so these children never go to school and they get teased a lot. The Ruel Foundation finds sponsors who help pay for the operations they need. You can choose which child you want to help on their website: www.ruelfoundation.com. It's so exciting! *The All for God Club* are going to choose a child and help pay for their operation. It will change their life!

The last few months have been so exciting. I know now why Jesus said, "It is more blessed to give than to receive."

The original All for God Club
L to R: Emily Boom, Marilie Van As, Aletia Van As and Eliza Boom

The Gift of Values

Think about it

- What was the girls' club motto?

- Why did Mum think that the money was God's gift to The All for God Club?

- Discuss the verse that says, "One man gives freely, yet gains even more; another withholds unduly, but comes to poverty. A generous man will prosper; he who refreshes others will himself be refreshed." *Proverbs 11: 24,25 NIV*

- What happens if we hoard money and refuse to give?

- Ask your children if they can remember a time when someone was generous towards them. How did they feel?

- What can we give besides money? (Some of the most precious gifts are not financial. It might be some baking, a helping hand, a load of firewood, a word of encouragement, a smile.)

- The other day I noticed a quote written on a blackboard outside a toy shop. Eliza scribbled it down for me as we drove past. 'Sharing is sometimes more demanding than giving." Discuss this. Is sharing a part of generosity? What can we share? With whom can we share? Encourage your little ones to share with their siblings and friends.

Boom Clip

I watched the girls' faces as they scoured the shop looking for things to put into their gift boxes for Fiji. What fun they had! And when I signed the cheque for them to buy the pig for the Cambodian family, their excitement made me feel jealous! That night, Chris and I had a good talk. We decided to start setting aside some money each fortnight into a family giving fund, which we would then all decide how to use.

Generosity

The very first family meeting in which we discussed the giving fund was fantastic. One of the children broke noodles into eight different lengths and we drew 'straws' to see who would chair the meeting. Milly won the honour. The rest of us ate our piece of noodle while she put on the Cat in the Hat hat and called the meeting to order. When she banged a spoon on a glass and said, "The meeting is here!" the hat slipped right down over her face. We all burst out laughing, and quick as a flash Josiah said, "The meeting is here, but where is Milly?" It was so much fun.

Everyone had their turn giving suggestions for using the money. It was a real thrill listening to the little ones give their ideas. Samuel said in a quiet voice, "I think we should buy a Bible for Linda." Linda was Chris's workmate who had just become a Christian. What a wonderful idea! All of us were filled with the joy of giving. What a fantastic evening! I just wish we'd started it years ago.

Something to do

- ❖ Talk with your children about any clubs you belonged to when you were a child. (When we lived as kids in Papua, New Guinea, Peter and Penny and I had a Jungle Club. To belong to it, we had to be able to run a set course through the jungle in a certain time; light a fire; use our bush knives; and climb a coconut tree. The other day, Milly, Sam and Jacob spent ages timing each other running across the meadow, swinging across the river on vines and other such things - "just like you did in New Guinea, eh Mum?")

- ❖ Brainstorm together about setting up a club. What makes a club work? Do you need to have a motto? There are so many fun things about having a club - passwords, secret codes etc. Talk with your children about the huge potential of clubs, both for good and for evil. Many clubs have been set up which are incredibly destructive, such as the Ku Klux Klan, motorcycle gangs, and Hitler Youth. Discuss with your

The Gift of Values

children the power of a group of people who believe the same thing and work together for a common goal. Challenge them to set up a club that will bring glory to God. Also you need to discuss the potential pitfalls of any club - squabbles, personality clashes, children feeling left out, arguments over who's going to be 'the boss', disagreements, and all sorts of incredibly complicated club issues!

- ❖ Get your older children to research the *Holy Club* set up by John and Charles Wesley and George Whitefield at Oxford University in the 1730's.

- ❖ If you can, let the children make a club house somewhere. Maybe they could spruce up an old shed out the back, tidy up a corner in the attic, or even make a tree hut!

- ❖ Be prepared to give your children some creative ideas and, if necessary, help them make things happen!

- ❖ Set up a family giving fund. You will never regret this. No matter if you can only set aside a small sum - remember the widow's mite!

- ❖ Think about some of the needs in the world today. Look up some of the relief agencies like World Vision, Tear Fund or ORA International and get ideas of projects for which the children could raise money.

- ❖ Encourage the children to do the World Vision 20 or 40 Hour Famine.

- ❖ Pocket money for doing chores is a wonderful way to teach children about money. Teach them right from the start how to tithe, give and save. I remember the day Eliza got her first pocket money when she was three. Her older brother and sister were doing the World Vision 20 Hour Famine for the first time and Eliza sponsored them both half a cent an hour each! So World vision received her very first pocket money of twenty cents.

- ❖ Read the following short story to your children.

Generosity

Lizzy's Quilt

When she was just thirteen, Lizzie injured her back in an accident. She spent the next 27 years flat on her back. Her only view of the world was from a mirror mounted above her head. Lizzie had always longed to make her life count for something worthwhile. When she was told that an African slave could be freed for $40, she made a quilt to sell for that price, but nobody would buy it. She then tried making bookmarks, and raised $1000 a year for each of her 27 years, and gave the money away to good projects.

One day a bishop from India was travelling through Illinois, and Lizzie gave him her quilt. He took it with him on his speaking tour around the country and wherever he went, he told the story of Lizzie. He asked people if they would place an offering for missions on the quilt. He raised $100,000! And every cent of it was the result of one girl's refusal to be limited by her sickness.

❖ Get the maths brain in your family to work out how much more money Lizzie's quilt actually raised for missions than the original price of $40. How much did she raise from her bookmarks and the quilt?

❖ Brainstorm together about what we can give besides money.

❖ Think of something that you could make as a family and sell to raise money for missions. Why not a quilt? Get each of your children to think of something they could make by themselves. There are books at the library that list countless creative ideas and ways that children can make money. You could also help the children sort through all their toys and books and see if there are any they might like to donate to a second-hand shop that gives its profits to a good cause.

❖ Read together and then act out the story of the little boy who offered his lunch to Jesus. (*John 6:9-13*) Discuss the truth that God always multiplies what we give Him.

Boom Clip

I recently spoke at a home schooling convention, and after my talk, a delightful six-year-old girl called Zara came to speak with me. She was fascinated by the book my children and I have produced to help raise money for a little girl in Zambia.

"I help poor people, too," she said.

"That's wonderful, Zara!" I said. "What do you do?"

She beamed at me. "I make jam with Grandma. We sell it and send the money to Africa. We've raised $1200 so far."

I could hardly believe my ears! "Really?" I said. "$1200? That's amazing!"

That's also a lot of jam! I feel tired just thinking about it.

How blessed God must be when He sees young children taking the initiative like that. But I couldn't help thinking that it's also taken a lot of support and commitment from Grandma to make it happen!

We need to get behind some of the ideas our children have and really encourage them in their efforts. I know that from experience. At the first few All for God Club cafes, parents and grandparents were the only ones who came and bought all the delectable delights our children had made. We paid to see the puppet shows and concerts. But what a fantastic way to spend some money!

So Said...

❖ "My rich dad said, 'Money does not make you rich.' He would go on to say that money has the power to make you either rich or poor… and for most people, the more money they make, the poorer they become." *Robert.T Kiyosaki*

❖ "No person was ever honoured for what he received. Honour has been the reward for what he gave." *Calvin Coolidge*

❖ "We make a living by what we get, but we make a life by what we give." *Winston Churchill*

❖ "My rich dad strongly encouraged his son and me to become rich by serving as many people as possible. He would say, 'When you focus your mind on making money only for yourself, you will find it difficult to become rich. If you are dishonest, greedy, and give people less than they pay for, you will also find it difficult to become rich. You can acquire wealth in those ways, but that wealth will come at a very high price. If you focus your business first on serving as many people as possible… think only of making their lives a little easier, you will find tremendous wealth and happiness.'" *Robert.T Kiyosaki*

❖ "The true meaning of life is to plant trees, under whose shade you do not expect to sit." *Nelson Henderson*

❖ "We should give as we would receive, cheerfully, quickly, and without hesitation; for there is no grace in a benefit that sticks to the fingers." *Seneca*

❖ "Think of giving not as a duty but as a privilege." *John D. Rockefeller Jr*

❖ "You have not lived today until you have done something for someone who can never repay you." *John Bunyan*

❖ "There is a wonderful mythical law of nature that the three things we crave most in life - happiness, freedom, and peace of mind - are always attained by giving them to someone else." *Peyton Conway March*

❖ "The more God gives you, the more responsible he expects you to be." *Rick Warren*

❖ "Real generosity is doing something nice for someone who will never find out." *Henry Ford*

❖ "Money is like an arm or leg - use it or lose it." *A. P. Gouthey*

The Gift of Values

❖ "Money never made a man happy yet, nor will it. There is nothing in its nature to produce happiness. The more a man has, the more he wants. Instead of filling a vacuum, it makes one." *William A. Ward*

❖ "Before you speak, listen. Before you write, think. Before you spend, earn. Before you invest, investigate. Before you criticize, wait. Before you pray, forgive. Before you quit, try. Before you retire, save. Before you die, give." *Anon*

❖ "A fool may make money, but it needs a wise man to spend it." *C.H. Spurgeon*

❖ "It is better to trust in work than money; God never buys anything and is forever at work." *George MacDonald*

Boom Clip

One morning at church, as I passed the offering pottle along the row, a thought struck me - something I'd never thought of before. I leaned over and asked Jacob, "Darling, do you know why Daddy and I never put money into the pottle?"

He shook his head. The older children all knew about automatic bank deposits, but not the younger ones. I realized then that they probably always thought we weren't giving anything. So I carefully explained to Jacob and Samuel about the blessing of tithing and giving, and automatic bank deposits!

Generosity

Words to live by

- "Remember this: Whoever sows sparingly will also reap sparingly, and whoever sows generously will also reap generously. Each man should give what he has decided in his heart to give, not reluctantly or under compulsion, for God loves a cheerful giver." *2 Corinthians 9:6 - 8 NIV*

- "Freely you have received, freely give." *Matthew 10:8 NIV*

- "… poor, yet making many rich; having nothing, and yet possessing everything." *2 Corinthians 6:10 NIV*

- "We have different gifts, according to the grace given us… if it is contributing to the needs of others, let him give generously." *Romans 12:6-8 NIV*

- "Then the King will say to those on His right, 'Come, you who are blessed by my Father; take your inheritance, the kingdom prepared for you since the creation of the world. For I was hungry and you gave me something to eat, I was thirsty and you gave me something to drink, I was a stranger and you invited me in, I needed clothes and you clothed me, I was sick and you looked after me, I was in prison and you came to visit me.' Then the righteous will answer him, 'Lord, when did we see you hungry and feed you, or thirsty and give you something to drink? When did we see you a stranger and invite you in, or needing clothes and clothe you? When did we see you sick or in prison and go to visit you? The King will reply, 'I tell you the truth, whatever you did for one of the least of these brothers of mine, you did it for me." *Matthew 25:34-40 NIV*

- "Give, and it will be given to you. A good measure, pressed down, shaken together and running over, will be poured into your lap. For with the measure you use, it will be measured to you." *Luke 6:38 NIV*

- "Command those who are rich in this present world not to be arrogant nor to put their hope in wealth, which is so uncertain, but to put their

The Gift of Values

hope in God, who richly provides us with everything for our enjoyment. Command them to do good, to be rich in good deeds, and to be generous and willing to share. In this way they will lay up treasure for themselves as a firm foundation for the coming age, so that they may take hold of the life that is truly life." *1 Timothy 6:17-20 NIV*

Dig deeper

- Read *The Sugar Creek Gang* books with your children.
- Read *The Famous Five books* and *The Secret Seven books* by Enid Blyton.
- Read *The Cambridge Seven* or *A Cambridge Movement* by J.C. Pollock. This group of seven earnest students from Cambridge University raised awareness of God amongst the university students. All seven of them went to China and served God there for different lengths of time. One of them, C.T Studd, gave away his fortune and went to serve God as a missionary in Africa. You can read his inspiring life story in: *C.T. Studd: Cricketer and Pioneer by Norman Grubb.*
- A good book for teenagers is *Student Volunteer Movement* by Charles Mott.
- Read *The Story of Johnny Appleseed* by Aliki with your younger children. Wherever John goes, he makes friends and leaves behind him a gift of apple trees.
- Read *The Giving Tree* by Shel Silverstein with your younger children. The tree and boy are best friends. As they grow older together, the tree provides the boy with what he needs at each of the different stages of his life.
- Amy Carmichael spent the last 30 years of her life confined to bed after an accident, but during that time she wrote countless books that blessed

and encouraged thousands. Encourage your older children to read one of the many biographies written about her.

- ❖ Read about George Mueller. There are countless books about this wonderful man who achieved so much because of his generous spirit. He built five large orphanages that cared for over 10,000 orphans. He gave over half a million dollars to school work; over one and a quarter million dollars to missionary work; and circulated nearly two million Bibles and three million books and tracts. In sixty years this man, who had no personal resources and who died with less than $300 to his name, had distributed about seven and a half million dollars! He was a giver extraordinaire!

- ❖ Read *The Bandit of Ashley Downs* by Dave and Neta Jackson. When Curly, a young homeless orphan, steals the money raised by a church for an orphanage, he is sent to the very orphanage he robbed. There, he is placed in the care of George Mueller.

The Gift of Values

The Silver Thread

In a far-flung corner of the kingdom of Straite, there lived a poor tailor and his beautiful daughter, Gabrielle. Her mother had died just after Gabrielle's seventh birthday, but not before she had taught her daughter how to sew with tiny, perfect stitches. For thirteen years no scissors had ever touched Gabrielle's head. Her golden hair fell long and straight down her back, and she sat on it as she sewed.

Every Saturday she went to the market with her father, where they traded their sewing for vegetables and fruit. They had no money, but they were rich in love.

"You are worth more to me than a kingdom of gold," her father told her morning and night.

One day, King William rode up to their cottage to view the clothes he had ordered the tailor to make for the Hunting Ball. When the tailor saw the king's entourage approaching his dwelling, his hands shook and he pricked his finger. A crimson drop fell on the embroidered silk.

"Fool!" cried the king. "Clumsy fool! You shall pay for this! Take him away," he cried to the guards. "Lock him in the castle until a ransom be paid."

"No, my Lord!" cried Gabrielle, falling to her knees on the dirt. "I beg you, have mercy. He is all I have in the world."

But the King paid her no heed, and rode off without a word.

That night Gabrielle sat alone by the window. She wanted to pray but could find no words amongst her tears. She lifted her face to the heavens. Silver moonlight streamed through the window and glistened on the tears that ran down her cheeks and into her hair.

The next morning she awoke and washed her face. Her swollen eyes ached. Her heart ached. She stood before the tin mirror and began to brush her hair.

After just three strokes, Gabrielle stopped in wonder. For shining amongst her golden hair, was a thread of purest silver.

With a swift pull, Gabrielle plucked it out. It was strong and straight, as fine a thread as any she had sewed with. She ran to fetch her sewing basket, threaded her smallest needle, and began to sew.

Dusk was falling when she reached the castle gates. "I bear a gift for the King," she said to the guards.

She trembled as she entered the grand hall and approached the throne. She curtsied low. "Please, your majesty, I bring you a gift in exchange for the release of my father, the tailor." And she held out a handkerchief in her slender trembling hands.

The King gasped. In the corner of the fine cotton was an elegant *W*, stitched in pure silver thread. "Tis the work of an angel!" he cried.

"Nay, Sire, for I made it with my own hand," said Gabrielle quietly.

"And where would a peasant girl such as yourself find so pure a thread?" growled the King.

Gabrielle looked down at the floor but spoke in a steady voice. "Tis hard to believe, Sire, but this very morning I found one thread of silver amongst my hair."

The king looked at his queen and then snorted. "And have you any of this thread left?"

"A little," replied Gabrielle.

The King thumped the velvet arm of his throne. "Splendid!" he cried. "Then you shall make me one more such handkerchief, initialed with the letter *S*. For Queen Sylbeth must have one also." Then with an impatient gesture, he signalled the guards, who marched Gabrielle from the hall.

All that night she sewed by the silver light of the moon. At dawn she made the long walk back to the castle.

"Is it not as I said?" cried the king to his queen, when Gabrielle presented them with the handkerchief. "Did you ever see such pure silver thread?"

"Such tiny, even stitches too," marvelled the queen.

The Gift of Values

"If it please, Your Majesty," began Gabrielle, "my father..."

"Silence!" shouted the king, for his heart had grown quite greedy. "You must bring me your spool of silver thread if your father is to be released."

"But I tell you the truth, Sire," cried Gabrielle. "There was only ever one thread of silver in my hair. I have used it all." And with that she began to cry.

"Enough!" bellowed the King. "How dare you withhold from your Lord! You shall rot with your father in my prison."

But at that very moment, the morning sun streamed through the window and lit upon Gabrielle's hair.

The King gasped. "Gold!" he cried, and his wicked heart swelled with greed. "Forget the silver, I shall have gold! Your father for your hair." He clapped his hands and ordered the guards to bring in the royal hairdresser.

When the hairdresser scuttled into the hall, Gabrielle bowed her head until her golden hair tumbled forward and touched the stone floor.

Snip. Snip. Snip. The scissors chopped and cut until all of Gabrielle's hair lay in a shimmering heap on the sun-drenched floor. The King rubbed his hands with glee. "Away with her," he said to his guards. "Fetch the tailor and send them from the castle."

And so it was, Gabrielle and her father escaped from the palace and made their way to a new country, while the greedy king searched in vain for any golden thread amongst Gabrielle's gift of hair.

Generosity

Think About It

- Were Gabrielle and her father rich? (No and yes!)
- Why did the king throw the tailor into prison?
- Discuss the quote, 'The greatest works of art are those made with love.'
- Why did the king suddenly change his mind, and decide to have Gabrielle's hair as a ransom?
- What is greed? Check some different definitions in a few dictionaries.
- What does greed do to us? (It corrupts our judgment. It blinds us to the truth. It tempts and seduces us from God's plan of giving.)
- Does greed ever leave us satisfied? (No, greed is a thief.)
- Discuss the saying, 'More will never be enough.'
- What was Gabrielle's gift?

Something To Do

- Get the children to write down a list of all the things they really want. Then go through it carefully, and discuss whether greed has crept in at all.
- Let the children try embroidering their initial on a handkerchief. Better still, make it the initial of someone they love, and make the hankie a gift.
- Discuss the lyrics in the song, *Beggars on the Road* by Penelope Foote. (My twin!) You may like to listen to it on our web site: *www.boomfamily.co.nz*

Beggars on the Road

Poverty has its riches and wealth is not all gain
There's many a rich man living a lonely life of pain
Don't set your heart on money 'cos it'll make itself wings and fly
And love of money's an evil that many have been ruined by

There are beggars on the road to glory,
Rich men who've lost their way
Don't make wealth your only friend 'cos she might never stay
Don't hold onto fortune's fingers 'cos she'll elude you by and by
Slip from your grasp and leave you, heedless of your cries

Money can't buy you freedom, can't buy you peace of mind
If you've got love and faith in God, a richer man you'll never find
Be content with what you've got, don't trade your soul for more
True riches are found in loving God and giving to the poor

A well-lined purse and money in the bank don't make for a happy life
There's many a rich man looking at a future of trouble and strife

There are beggars on the road to glory,
Rich men who've lost their way
Don't make wealth your only friend 'cos she might never stay
Don't hold onto fortune's fingers 'cos she'll elude you by and by
Slip from your grasp and leave you, heedless of your cries

- ❖ After I'd written this chapter I discovered a children's book in the library called *The Gift* by Bob J. Bernreuter. It tells the story of a princess with long red hair. One day she meets a young girl in her kingdom who has no hair at all. She decides to do something to help her. She cuts off her hair and takes it to the wig maker who creates a beautiful wig for the girl. In the back of the book, the author writes about the charitable organization *Locks of Love*, which provides hairpieces to children who have long-term medical hair loss. We visited the web site (*www.locksoflove.org*) and watched the video clip describing how you can donate your long hair. Inspiring! Milly decided there and then that she wanted to cut off her long hair and send it to them! What a wonderful blessing. Maybe one of your daughters will also become inspired and make the gift of her hair? As it says on the *Locks of Love* web site, 'The gift of hair is priceless, is renewable, and will only cost you a little pride.'

So Said...

- ❖ "Earth provides enough to satisfy every man's need, but not every man's greed.' *Mahatma Gandhi*
- ❖ "A greedy father has thieves for children." *Serbian Proverb*
- ❖ "If you're not greedy, you will go far, you will live in happiness too, like the oompa loompa doompity do." *Charlie and the Chocolate Factory.*
- ❖ "He who is greedy is always in want." *Horace*
- ❖ A Native American grandfather talking with his young grandson tells the boy he has two wolves inside him, struggling with each other. The first is the wolf of peace, love and kindness. The other wolf is fear, greed and hatred. "Which wolf will win, Grandfather?" asks the young boy. "Whichever one I feed," replies the grandfather. *North American Proverb*

The Gift of Values

- ❖ "The man who has won millions at the cost of his conscience is a failure." *B C. Forbes*

- ❖ "If your thinking is sloppy, your business will be sloppy. If you are disorganized, your business will be disorganized. If you are greedy, your employees will be greedy, giving you less and less of themselves and always asking for more." *Michael Gerber*

- ❖ "It is not the man who has little, but he who desires more, that is poor." *Seneca*

- ❖ "It is a great blessing to possess what one wishes," said one to an ancient philosopher, who replied, "It is a greater blessing still, not to desire what one does not possess." *Wm.M.Thayer*

Boom Clip

Tears streamed down my face as I said my last goodbye to my friends in Borneo. They gave me a beautiful book about the Iban people and $140 - a fortune to a poor missionary girl!

The next day, I scoured the shops in Singapore, searching for something special to buy with the money as a memento. Finally, I bought a book for $10 and decided to hold onto the rest of the money until I saw something I really wanted.

The following day, I caught a bus to Kuala Lumpur to visit a friend of mine from New Zealand who had been imprisoned for preaching the Gospel to a Muslim. There was a lot of jostling and pushing as people fought to get on the bus, and it wasn't until I sat down and looked for my tickets that I realized I had been robbed! All my money and travellers cheques - gone. I sat there shocked. Then, unbidden, a thought flashed into my mind. *Rats! If only I'd spent all the money!* Seconds later, another thought followed hard on its heels. *This is how people will feel when they stand before God and realize they should have 'spent' their money by giving when they had the opportunity.*

Generosity

I realised then that none of us will ever regret the money we've given. Our regret will be that we didn't give more. I wrote the song *Riches to Rust* shortly after this.

On a pavement in Rangoon
In the blistering noonday sun
Lies a tiny little baby
Near the place where tourists come
And her mother points towards her
And holds out her hand
Imploring every stranger
As they pass by

In a village high in Thailand
Where the opium flower grows
There's a one-roomed hut
And a dusty pile of clothes
And shame fills my heart
As the memory floods my mind
Of the money I have squandered
On some latest fashion find

Silver and gold
Covered with rust
All of those clothes eaten by moths
So many opportunities
To bless, to give, and to love
To give away riches on earth
Is to store up treasures above

In Kathmandu a beggar
With deformed and twisted legs
Drags himself along
On a makeshift rubber sledge
He begs you for some money
Just to buy a simple meal
A bowl of rice for a few rupees
Would help him in his need

But you say 'we have no money
We couldn't possibly give!
Why we're struggling
Just to find the cash
To pay the latest bills
Our TV's on hire purchase
The new video is too
Our credit card bill is ten feet long
And payment's almost due!'

Silver and gold
Covered with rust
All of those clothes eaten by moths
So many opportunities
To bless, to give, and to love
To give away riches on earth
Is to store up treasures above

(You can listen to this song on our web site *www.boomfamily.co.nz*).

Words To Live By

- "And he said to them, 'Beware, and be on your guard against every form of greed; for not even when one has an abundance does his life consist of his possessions.'" *Luke 12:15 NASB*

- "But godliness actually is a means of great gain, when accompanied by contentment. For we have brought nothing into the world, so we cannot take anything out of it either. And if we have food and covering, with these we shall be content. But those who want to get rich fall into temptation and a snare and many foolish and harmful desires which plunge men into ruin and destruction. For the love of money is a root of all sorts of evil, and some by longing for it have wandered away from the faith, and pierced themselves with many a pang." *1 Timothy 6:6-10 NASB*

- "Do not weary yourself to gain wealth, cease from your consideration of it. When you set your eyes on it, it is gone. For wealth certainly makes itself wings, like an eagle that flies towards heaven." *Proverbs 23:4,5 NASB*

- "The graven images of their gods you are to burn with fire; you shall not covet the silver or the gold that is on them, nor take it for yourselves, lest you be snared by it, for it is an abomination to the Lord your God." *Deuteronomy 7:25 NASB*

- "…not greedy for money, but eager to serve." *1 Peter 5: 3 NIV*

- "But mark this: There will be terrible times in the last days. People will be lovers of themselves, lovers of money, boastful, proud, abusive, disobedient to their parents, ungrateful, unholy, without love, unforgiving, slanderous, without self-control, brutal, not lovers of the good, treacherous, rash, conceited, lovers of pleasure rather than lovers of God - having a form of godliness but denying its power." *2 Timothy 3:1 - 5 NIV*

Generosity

- "If there is a poor man with you, one of your brothers, in any of your towns in your land which the Lord your God is giving you, you shall not harden your heart, nor close your hand from your poor brother; but you shall freely open your hand to him, and shall generously lend him sufficient for his need in whatever he lacks. Beware, lest there is a base thought in your heart, saying, 'The seventh year, the year of remission is near,' and your eye is hostile toward your poor brother, and you give him nothing; then he may cry to the Lord against you, and it will be a sin in you. You shall generously give to him, and your heart shall not be grieved when you give to him, because for this thing the Lord your God will bless you in all your work and in all your undertakings. For the poor will never cease to be in the land; therefore I command you, saying, 'You shall freely open your hand to your brother, to your needy and poor in your land.'" *Deuteronomy 15:7 - 11 NASB*

- "Better a dinner of herbs where love is, than a fattened ox and hatred therewith." *Proverbs 17:1 K.J.V*

The Gift of Values

Dig Deeper

- ❖ Read *Little Women* or watch the DVD. Jo cuts off all her hair to raise money to help her father. When Amy sees it, she cries, "Jo! Your one beauty!"

- ❖ Read about two greedy men in the Bible: Gehazi (*2 Kings chapter 5*) and Judas. (*John 12:1 - 6*)

- ❖ Read Leo Tolstoy's short story, *How Much Land Does a Man Need?* In this classic tale, Tolstoy teaches an important lesson about contentment and the terrible consequences of greed.

- ❖ Read *The Necklace* by Guy de Maupassant. Madame Loisel always longed for the fine things that her rich friends enjoy. But her envy exacts a high price.

- ❖ Read *A Christmas Carol* with your younger children. It's a powerful tale of the greedy Ebenezer Scrooge, and how he comes to recognize what makes men truly rich, and the joy of giving.

The Box

(Each time I read this story, I am moved to tears. I think perhaps it's the author's truthful unveiling of the thoughts of her heart during one of life's darkest moments that touches me most. I have tried to trace the author of this story but with no success. I hope she would be pleased for me to retell it in this book, knowing that many more hearts will be blessed with the wonderful story of God's provision.)

I remember a day one winter that stands out like a boulder in my life. The weather was unusually cold, our salary had not been regularly paid, and it did not meet our needs when it was. My husband was away much of the time, travelling from one district to another. Our boys were well, but my little Ruth was ailing, and at best none of us were decently clothed. I patched and re-patched, with spirits sinking to the lowest ebb. The water gave out in the well, and the wind blew through the cracks in the floor.

The people in the parish were kind and generous too; but the settlement was new, and each family was struggling for itself. Little by little, at the time I needed it most, my faith began to waver.

Early in life I was taught to take God at His word, and I thought my lesson was well learned. I had lived upon His promises in dark times, until I knew, as David did, "who was my Fortress and Deliverer." Now a daily prayer for forgiveness was all that I could offer.

My husband's overcoat was hardly thick enough for October, and he was often obliged to ride miles to attend some meeting or funeral. Many times our breakfast was Indian cake, and a cup of tea without sugar. Christmas was coming; the children always expecting presents. I remember the ice was thick and smooth, and the boys were each craving a pair of skates. Ruth, in some unaccountable way, had taken a fancy that the dolls I had made were no longer suitable; she wanted a nice large one, and insisted on praying for it. I knew it seemed impossible, but oh! I wanted so very much to give the

The Gift of Values

children the presents they each longed for. It seemed as if God had deserted us, but I did not tell my husband all this. He worked so earnestly and heartily. I supposed him to be as hopeful as ever. I kept the sitting room cheerful with an open fire and tried to serve our scanty meals as appealingly as I could.

The morning before Christmas, James was called in to see a sick man. I put up a piece of bread for his lunch - it was the best I could do - wrapped my plaid shawl around his neck, and then tried to whisper a promise as I often had, but the words died away upon my lips. I let him go without it.

That was a dark, hopeless day. I coaxed the children to bed early, for I could not bear their talk. When Ruth went to bed, I listened to her prayer. She asked for the last time most explicitly for her doll, and for the skates for her brothers. Her bright face looked so lovely when she whispered to me, "You know I think they'll be here early tomorrow morning, Mama." I thought then that I would move heaven and earth to save her from the disappointment. I sat down alone that night and gave way to the most bitter tears.

Before long James returned, chilled and exhausted. He drew off his boots; the thin stockings slipped off with them and his feet were red with cold.

"I wouldn't treat a dog this way, let alone a faithful servant!" I said bitterly. Then as I glanced up and saw the hard lines in his face and the look of despair, it flashed across me - James had let go, too.

I brought him a cup of tea, feeling sick and dizzy at the very thought. He took my hand and we sat for an hour without a word. I wanted to die and meet God, and tell Him His promise wasn't true; my soul was so full of rebellious despair.

There came a sound of bells, a quick stop, and a loud knock at the door. James sprang up to open it. There stood Deacon White.

"A box came by express just before dark," he said. "I brought it round as soon as I could get away. Reckon it might be for Christmas. 'At any rate,' I said, 'they shall have it tonight.' Here is a turkey my wife asked me to fetch along, and these other things I believe belong to you."

There was a basket of potatoes and a bag of flour. Talking all the time, he carried in a box, and then, with a hearty goodnight, he rode away.

Still without speaking, James found a chisel and opened the box. He drew out first a thick red blanket, and saw that beneath was full of clothing. It seemed at that moment as if Christ fastened on me a look of reproach. James sat down and covered his face with his hands. "I cannot touch them," he exclaimed; "I haven't been true, just when God was trying me to see if I could hold out. Do you think I could not see how you were suffering? And I had no word of comfort to offer. I know now how to preach the awfulness of turning from God."

"James," I said, clinging to him, "don't take it to heart like this; I am to blame, I ought to have helped you. We will ask Him together to forgive us."

"Wait a moment, dear, I cannot talk now," he said, then he went into another room. I knelt down, and my heart broke; in an instant all the darkness, all the stubbornness rolled away. Jesus came again and stood before me, but with the loving word: "Daughter!"

Sweet promises of tenderness and joy flooded my soul. I was so lost in praise and gratitude that I forgot everything else. I don't know how long it was before James came back, but I knew he, too, had found peace.

"Now, my dear wife," he said, "let us thank God together." He then poured out words of praise; Bible words, for nothing else could express our thanksgiving.

It was 11 o'clock, the fire was low, and there was the great box, and nothing touched but the warm blanket we had so desperately needed. We piled on some fresh logs, lighted two candles, and began to examine our treasures.

We drew out an overcoat; I made James try it on. It was just the right size and I danced around him, for all my lightheartedness had returned.

There was a warm suit of clothes also, and three pairs of woollen hose. There was a dress for me, and yards of flannel; a pair of arctic overshoes for each of us, and in mine was a slip of paper. I have it now, and mean to hand it down to my children. It was Jacob's blessing to Asher, "Thy shoes shall be iron and brass, and as thy days, so shall thy strength be." In the gloves,

The Gift of Values

evidently for James, the same dear hand had written, "I, the Lord thy God, will hold thy right hand, saying unto thee, 'Fear not, I will help thee.'"

It was a wonderful box, and packed with thoughtful care. There was a suit of clothes for each of the boys and a little red gown for Ruth. There were mittens, scarves, and hoods; and down in the center, a box. We opened it and there was a great wax doll. I burst into tears again; James wept with me for joy. It was too much; and then we both exclaimed again, for next we drew out two pairs of skates. There were books for us to read; some of them I had wished to see; stories for the children to read; aprons and underclothing; yards of ribbon; a lovely photograph; needles, buttons and thread; and an envelope containing a ten-dollar gold piece.

At last we cried over everything we took up. It was past midnight, and we were faint and exhausted with happiness. I made a cup of tea, cut a fresh loaf of bread and James boiled some eggs. We drew up the table before the fire - how we enjoyed our supper! And then we sat talking over our life, and how sure a help God always proved to be.

You should have seen the children the next morning. The boys raised a shout at the sight of their skates. Ruth caught up her doll, and hugged it tightly without a word. Then she went into her room and knelt by her bed.

When she came back she whispered to me, "I knew it would be there, Mama, but I wanted to thank God just the same, you know."

"Look here, wife," cried James. We went to the window and there were the boys out of the house already, and skating on the ice with all their might.

My husband and I both tried to return thanks to the church in the East that sent us the box and have tried to return thanks unto God every day since.

Hard times have come again and again, but we have trusted in Him; dreading nothing so much as a doubt of His protecting care. Over and over again we have proved that, "They that seek the Lord shall not want any good thing."

Think About It

- ❖ See if your children can remember everything that was in the box.

- ❖ The gift of the box gave more than just physical gifts to the receivers. What else did it offer the family? (Hope; the assurance that God loved them and had heard their prayers; the knowledge that someone cared for them; the promises for future provision that were tucked inside the shoes and gloves.)

- ❖ The author uses the expression, "the same dear hand had written…" Discuss this.

- ❖ What words did the author use to describe how the box had been packed? (Thoughtfully.) Talk about gifts that are given prayerfully, carefully, and thoughtfully, as opposed to expensive gifts that are merely tokens.

- ❖ The sentiment and love that prompts the gift is much more important than the gift itself. Get each child to share about a gift they have received which was more valuable to them than the gift itself.

- ❖ The biggest gifts are not always the most valuable. Ask your children to think of a small gift that meant more to them than large, expensive ones that they've received.

Boom Clip

The children woke up feeling excited. Today we were going to help Penny and David, my sister and her husband, harvest their olives. School was called off for the day. We sang the old chorus as we worked, "Though the fig tree does not blossom and there be no fruit on the vines; the produce of the olive fails and the fields yield no food; though the flock be cut off from the fold and there be no herd in the stall; yet will I rejoice in the Lord, yet will I rejoice in the Lord. I will joy in the God of my salvation; God the Lord is my strength." *(Habakkuk 3:17, 18)* It was a wonderful time, all working together.

The Gift of Values

At the end of the day, Samuel came to me and said in a gentle voice, "Mummy, this is for you." Lying in the palm of his hand was a tiny cross that he had carved out of olive wood with his pocket knife. What a beautiful gift. I will treasure it forever.

Something To Do

- Get each child to pray and ask the Lord to give them an idea of how they can bless someone with a special gift. Encourage them to hand make the gift. A plate of cookies, or a loaf of fresh warm bread would be a wonderful gift for the old couple who live down the road.

- Play *Angels and Mortals*. This is a favourite game in our family. Each person writes their name on a piece of paper and puts it in a hat. Then you each draw out a name. This person then becomes your 'mortal'. You will be their unknown angel for a week. The object of the game is to secretly bless your mortal each day, without them guessing who their angel is. It's so much fun as you each try and think of new, creative ways you can bless your mortal, without them seeing you or guessing who you are. At the end of the week, there is the great unveiling as each person guesses who their angel is! The game really encourages the children to think carefully about what they can do for their mortal. If their mortal is a boy, they probably won't appreciate the little bunch of buttercups on their pillow as much as Mummy will. I love the glowing look on my child's face when she runs out of my bedroom and says, "Mummy! I just heard the flutter of wings!" And there on my bed is a little bookmark, with twenty cents cellotaped onto it and a very tender note from my 'angle.' One of the funniest was signed, "Love from your chubby cheribum." I think they meant cherubim!

- Read together the account of Peter and the crippled beggar outside the temple gate. The beggar wants money, but Peter gives him something worth much more than that. "Silver and gold I do not have, but what

I have, I give you. In the name of Jesus Christ of Nazareth, walk." *Acts 3:1-9 NIV* This is a great passage to discuss. We may not have silver and gold, but that doesn't mean we can't be givers. We have something infinitely more valuable. The greatest gifts will never be measured in money. This particular story has been one of the Boom favourites to act out. We always end the play by singing the old chorus, and leaping about the room, like the beggar. "And he went walking and leaping and praising God…"

So Said…

- "You can give without loving, but you can never love without giving." *Robert Louis Stevenson*

- "Let us not be satisfied with just giving money. Money is not enough, money can be got, but they need your hearts to love them. So, spread your love everywhere you go." *Mother Teresa*

- "Generosity consists not in the sum given, but the manner in which it is bestowed." *Anon*

- "Make no mistake, my friend, it takes more than money to make men rich." *Benjamin Franklin*

- "What I spent is gone, what I kept, is lost, but what I gave away will be mine forever." *Ethel Percy Andrus*

- "If you can't feed a hundred people then just feed one." *Mother Teresa*

- "If you have much, give of your wealth, if you have little, give of your heart." *Arab Proverb*

- "The value of a man lies in what he gives and not in what he is capable of receiving." *Albert Einstein*

- "The manner of giving is worth more than the gift." *Pierre Corneille*

The Gift of Values

- ❖ "Do all the good you can, by all the means you can, in all the ways you can, in all the places you can, at all the times you can, to all the people you can, as long as you ever can." *John Wesley*
- ❖ "What you are is God's gift to you; what you do with yourself is your gift to God." *Danish Proverb*
- ❖ "The greatest gift you can give someone is your time." *Rick Warren*
- ❖ "Think of giving not as a duty but as a privilege." *D. Rockefeller Jr*
- ❖ "Do something for somebody every day for which you do not get paid." *Albert Schweitzer*

Boom Clip

When the storm hit us, we had four months of rain in two weeks. Gale force winds battered our barn, and Chris spent long, cold, wet hours outside in the elements trying to secure the place, rescue stock, dig drains and a hundred other things. He came in exhausted one evening and sat by the fire. I got some cream and began to massage his rough, cracked hands. When Eliza saw me doing that, she offered to give her father a 'proper' hand massage. She made up a mixture of sugar and olive oil and began to massage it in. After some time, Chris said to her, "They feel wonderful! And I'll bet your hands feel great, too."

"Yep," said Eliza. "They sure do!"

When I heard her say that, I realised we had just witnessed a wonderful example of the blessings of generosity. Every time you bless others, and are generous, you can't help but share the blessing!

Words To Live By

- "Do not be deceived: God cannot be mocked. A man reaps what he sows. The one who sows to please his sinful nature, from that nature will reap destruction; the one who sows to please the Spirit, from the Spirit will reap eternal life. Let us not become weary in doing good, for at the proper time we will reap a harvest if we do not give up. Therefore, as we have opportunity, let us do good to all people, especially to those who belong to the family of believers." *Galations 6:7 - 10 NIV*

- "Sell your possessions and give to the poor. Provide purses for yourselves that will not wear out, a treasure in heaven that will not be exhausted, where no thief comes near and no moth destroys. For where your treasure is, there will your heart be also." *Luke 12:32 - 34 NIV*

- "As he looked up, Jesus saw the rich putting their gifts into the temple treasury. He also saw a poor widow put in two very small copper coins. "I tell you the truth," he said, "this poor widow has put in more than all the others. All these people gave their gifts out of their wealth; but she out of her poverty put in all she had to live on.'" *Luke 21:1-4 NIV*

- "And now, brothers, we want you to know about the grace that God has given the Macedonian churches. Out of the most severe trial, their overflowing joy and their extreme poverty welled up in rich generosity. For I testify that they gave as much as they were able and even beyond their ability." *2 Corinthians 12:1-3 NIV*

- "One man gives freely, yet gains even more; another withholds unduly, but comes to poverty. A generous man will prosper; he who refreshes others, will himself be refreshed." *Proverbs 11:24,25 NIV*

The Gift of Values

❖ "Give, and it will be given to you. A good measure, pressed down, shaken together and running over, will be poured into your lap. For with the measure you use, it will be measured to you." *Luke 6:38 NIV*

❖ "No matter what I say, what I believe, I am bankrupt without love." *1 Corinthians 13:1 MSG*

Boom Clip

The children were excited about our trip to town. We were going to buy an electric frying pan for some friends of ours who really needed one.

We had fun looking at all the different models, while I kept a careful eye on the price tags. One particular model was considerably bigger than all the rest, and I knew that it was the pick of the bunch for this big family. But it was considerably more expensive. As I picked up a smaller model, I felt a gentle prompting to put it down and buy the biggest one. I looked at the price again. It was $40 extra. I hesitated for a moment, and then decided to obey.

"We'll take this one, please," I said to the shop attendant.

He made a quick search and then said, "I'm sorry, but we seem to have run out of that particular model. I don't suppose you'd like to buy the display model? I could give you a good discount on it."

Too right I would!

The children and I walked out of the shop with the biggest and best frypan, and we'd paid less for it than the one the next size down!

"See, kids!" I exclaimed. "God blessed us because we wanted to bless someone else."

They were all excited about it. But there was more to come! I had one more errand to do. I needed some clip-on sunglasses for my glasses. I told the children to wait in the car, and went inside the optometrist shop where the Boom family all get their glasses. The shop owner showed me a number of different styles, all of them over $50. I told him it was more than I wanted to spend. At that moment, he clipped on a pair that fitted perfectly.

"Here you are, Rose," he said. "This pair fits perfectly. You can have these ones." I asked him how much they cost, and he shook his head and said, "No, you can just have them." I couldn't believe my ears! When I protested, he smiled at me and said, "Don't argue! I'm allowed to give away something if I want to."

I couldn't wait to get out to the car and show the children! What a wonderful example it was to us of God's promise. "Give and it will be given to you. A good measure, pressed down and running over, will be poured into your lap. For with the measure you use, it will be measured to you." *Luke 6:38 NIV*

Dig Deeper

- ❖ Read about Hudson Taylor's good friend, William Thomas Berger, who supported him faithfully throughout all the years Hudson was in China.

- ❖ Watch the DVD *Silas Marner* or read the book by George Eliot. After suffering betrayal and rejection, Silas Marner leaves his community to settle in a strange place. There the lonely weaver becomes obsessed with accumulating money, until one day a little golden-haired orphan girl wanders into his home.

- ❖ Read *Christy* by Catherine Marshall. Christy is only nineteen years old when she leaves home to teach school at a mission in the Smoky Mountains. She longs to help the people, but finds them very loath to receive anything that smells of 'charity'. Christy writes letters back home and receives boxes of gifts for the mountain people, but they will have nothing to do with them. Christy discovers the greatest gift she has ever offered them is her love and friendship. Also available on DVD. We've enjoyed watching them as a family.

The Gift of Values

- ❖ The film *Les Miserables* is one of my favourites. When the bishop takes pity on Jean Valjean, he inspires him to a life of integrity by his generosity. Valjean shows the same generosity of spirit in all his later dealings with the poor.

- ❖ Read *The Quiltmaker's Gift* by Jeff Brumbeau. The rich and greedy king demands a quilt from the quilt maker. She explains to him that each of her quilts is given only to a needy person, and she refuses to give him one. Finally the king discovers that happiness is found in giving, not grabbing. Beautifully illustrated for younger children.

- ❖ Read *Miss Fannie's Hat* by Toni Goffe. Miss Fannie has a closet full of hats and loves each one. When the church decides to have an auction to raise money, Miss Fannie makes the difficult decision to give her favourite hat - the one she's worn each Easter Sunday for 35 years!

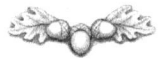

Value Two

ENCOURAGEMENT

A little boy begged his dad to come outside and play darts with him. He told his father, "I'll throw and you say, "Wonderful!"

Are you smiling? I was when I read that story. My own children have said similar things. To be absolutely honest, *I've* said similar things. It's not just children that need encouragement. We all need affirmation and approval. We all need someone who will stand beside us and tell us that we're doing O.K. Someone who believes in us. Someone who will encourage us.

There are few things more uplifting and inspiring than having someone who loves you cheering you on, applauding your attempts and encouraging you to try again. Conversely, it is hard to thrive when you feel that no matter what you do, it's never quite good enough. Criticism is very destructive. If all a child hears is, 'What a lousy throw!' he will soon stop picking up the dart at all.

As parents, we have dozens of opportunities each day to say, "Wonderful!" to our children. We need to be lavish with our encouragement. We should look for any opportunity to say, "Well done!" If your five-year-old has done his best to tidy his room, make sure he knows you're proud of him. If there are still a few toys and dirty socks scattered on the floor, never mind. Encourage him with what he has done, and help him finish the job. He'll try even harder to please you next time.

The Gift of Values

One of the joys of being a parent is being invited by your child to 'throw darts' with him. Don't miss the game by being too busy or too distracted. And remember, it doesn't have to be a bull's eye for you to shout, 'Wonderful!'

I was raised in a home where encouragement was our daily bread, and I am so thankful to God for that. I grew up feeling loved, and with a healthy confidence in myself, but even more importantly, in God. I suppose in many ways I took it for granted. But I soon realised that not everybody had such supportive and encouraging parents. I watched friends struggle with low self-esteem, which stemmed directly from the cutting, negative comments that their parents threw at them constantly. I watched them try to rise to the challenge of a career, or serving the Lord in some capacity, all the while trying to shake off the negative words spoken over them as children.

The word 'encouragement' means 'to fill with courage.' In the book of Job it says, "Your words have supported those who stumbled; you have strengthened faltering knees." *(Job 4:3,4 NIV)* A few simple words can inject courage and strength into a broken heart.

I long for each of my children to be encouragers. I know that some of them naturally tend that way, but I want *all* of them to learn how to be encouragers. I also want them to know how to encourage their own hearts. They won't always have someone beside them to pick them up when they're down.

I remember one of my pastors saying, "I am a pessimist by nature, but I've become a trained optimist." Exactly! I want my children to become *trained* encouragers. That way, when they become parents, they will speak encouragement into the hearts and lives of their children.

We all need encouragement, and we can all give it. My prayer is that as you read this chapter, you will commit to filling your home with encouragement, and that you will teach your children how to become encouragers. Often, it is just plain, ugly old habit that makes us say the things we do. The words are out of our mouths before we've even thought about them. We need to train ourselves to stop and think before we speak, and then to choose words that will build up and not tear down. Trained encouragers.

☙

The Castle of Giant Despair

Adapted from the story Pilgrim's Progress by John Bunyan

Hopeful stooped to pick a stone out of his shoe. "The way is rough, indeed," he said to his companion.

Christian nodded and sat down on the roots of a large spreading tree to rub his weary feet. Hopeful came and sat beside him. "We have need of perseverance, brother. We will reach the Celestial City if we faint not."

"Yes," replied Christian, "but do you see that meadow, Hopeful? Come. Let us take a look. There is a stile into the meadow to the left of our road." He got up and made his way over to the meadow. "Aha!" cried Christian. "It is just as I hoped! There lies a pleasant, easy path in the meadow, right beside our way. Come, good Hopeful, let us cross the stile and walk for a while on an easier path."

"But what if this path should lead us out of the way?" said Hopeful.

"That is not likely," replied Christian. "Look, it follows our road."

And so, with this persuasion, Hopeful followed his friend over the stile and into the meadow. The new path was very pleasant. They had not traveled long, before they caught sight of a fellow traveler on the path ahead of them. "Ho!" cried Christian. "What is your name and where are you headed?"

"My name is Vain-Confidence," said the man, "and I am bound for the Celestial City."

"What did I tell you, Hopeful?" cried Christian, clapping his hands. "By this we can be sure we are on the right way."

They fell in behind the man until the night grew dark and hid him from their sight.

Then they heard a fearful sound, as Vain-Confidence fell into a deep pit.

Hopeful called out to him. "What has happened? Are you alright?"

But there was no answer.

The Gift of Values

Hopeful turned a worried face to Christian. "Where are we, brother?" But Christian was silent. Uneasy thoughts began to creep into his mind.

And then it began to rain. Thunder and lightning crashed and flashed around them in a dreadful manner.

"Oh!" groaned Hopeful. "If only I had kept on the way."

"Who would have thought that this path should have led us out of the way?" answered Christian.

"I was afraid about it at the very start," said Hopeful. "I would have spoken plainer, but you are older than I."

"Forgive me, brother!" cried Christian. "I am so sorry I have led you out of the way, and placed you in such grave danger. Surely, I meant you no harm!"

"Take comfort, Christian, for I forgive you. And I believe that even this shall turn out for our good."

Christian embraced his friend. "How glad I am that I have a merciful brother. Now come, let us try to return to the path."

But try as they may, they could not find the stile. Finally, the two travelers settled beneath some shelter and fell into an exhausted sleep.

Christian winced as a huge boot kicked him in the side. "Wake up!" snarled a grim voice. "Who is this that dares to travel through my land?"

The two companions looked up at the huge, ugly giant that towered above them. At last Hopeful found his voice. "We are pilgrims, sir, and have lost our way."

"Well, you have this night trespassed on me," roared the giant, "and trampled my grounds. Now you must come with me." And with that, he forced them to their feet and drove them like cattle before him to Doubting Castle. Here, he threw them into a dungeon so vile, so dark, that the two companions grew terrified. The heavy door clanged shut and the key turned in the massive iron lock.

"Alas!" cried Christian. "Mine is the double sorrow, for I have brought this upon us by my own foolishness."

For three days Christian and Hopeful languished in the dark, stinking prison. Giant Despair gave them neither food nor drink. Each day he took his crab-tree club and beat them mercilessly. And every night, at his wife's suggestion, he left in their cell a rope, a knife and some poison. "Why should you choose to live," he taunted, "when life is so bitter? See, I offer you a choice!" And with a cruel laugh he locked the door and shut out all light from their cell.

"What shall we do, brother?" moaned Christian. "Perhaps the giant is right? This life we now live is miserable indeed. My soul chooses hanging rather than life. The grave is easier for me than this dungeon."

"Not so!" cried Hopeful. "Do not say such things. Not everything is in the hands of Giant Despair! Perhaps the giant will fall into one of his fits, or forget to lock the door. Yes, our present condition is dreadful, and death would be more welcome to me also than this dungeon. But the Lord of the country to which we go has said, 'You shall do no murder. Whatever we do, Christian, let us not become our own murderers!"

And in this way Hopeful moderated the mind of his brother.

That evening, the Giant went down to the dungeon to see if his prisoners had taken his counsel. When he saw them still alive, he fell into a rage and shouted, "It shall be worse for you than if you'd never been born."

At these words Christian fell into a swoon. When he came to, the giant was gone and Hopeful knelt at his side. "Fear not, Christian," he said. "Do you not remember how valiant you have been up until now? Apollyon could not crush you, nor could all that you did see and hear and feel in the Valley of the Shadow of Death. Remember how you stood as a brave man at Vanity Fair, and were neither afraid of the chain, nor the cage, nor even death. What hardship and terror you have already come through! And now, will you give way to your fears? Behold, I am in the dungeon with you, a far weaker man by nature than you. I, too, have had nothing to eat or drink. I also mourn without the light. But come, brother! Let us exercise a little more patience. We shall endure this."

The Gift of Values

That night, Giant Despair's wife asked him if the prisoners had yet taken his counsel and ended their lives.

"They are sturdy rogues," he answered. "They choose rather to bear all hardships than make away with themselves."

"Then," said she, "take them into the castle-yard tomorrow, and show them the bones and skulls of other travelers you have killed. Make them believe that when the week comes to an end, you will tear them into pieces, as you have done to others before them."

So, when the morning was come, the two friends saw a terrible sight, and heard the Giant's dreadful threats.

That night, as they sat together in the dark, they began to pray, and continued in prayer till almost break of day. Now, a little before dawn, Christian leaped to his feet and shouted, "What a fool I am, to lie here in this stinking dungeon when we can go free! I have a key in my possession, called Promise, which surely will open any door in Doubting Castle." And he reached in his shirt and pulled out a key, which was hanging around his neck - the key of Promise.

"Try it!" said Hopeful, hopefully.

The dungeon door flew open with ease, and the two friends crept out of the dungeon and up to the outer iron gate. That too, creaked open and, without sparing a backward glance, Christian and Hopeful fled from Doubting Castle, back to the true path.

When once they found the stile, they erected a pillar and wrote upon its side:

Over this stile is the way to Doubting Castle, which is kept by Giant Despair, who despises the King of the Celestial Country, and seeks to destroy his holy pilgrims.

Many, therefore, that followed after them, read what was written and escaped the terrible danger of Doubting Castle.

Think About It

- Where were the two pilgrims heading to?

- Why did they leave the given road?

- Whose idea was it?

- What difficulties and trials did they face in Giant Despair's dungeon?

- When Christian felt so despairing that he considered taking his own life, how did Hopeful dissuade him?

- What does the expression, 'moderated the mind of his brother' mean?

- How else did Hopeful encourage his fearful friend? (He reminded him of past victories; he spoke of potential ways of deliverance; he prayed with him.)

- Discuss the line, "Not everything is in the hands of Giant Despair."

- How did they finally escape from Doubting Castle?

Boom Clip

Milly was so excited! It was her very first time competing in the Weet-Bix Tryathlon. (A triathlon especially for young children.) The whole family went along to cheer for her. I felt really nervous as I watched her dive into the pool with scores of other children. The pool became a mess of thrashing, surging arms and legs. I nearly cried when I saw the first child emerge, and realized it was my daughter. She did a quick changeover for the bike leg of the race, and was off in a flash. When we saw her again at the end of that leg, I could tell she was exhausted.

The Gift of Values

You can do it, Milly!" shouted Kate, as Milly pulled off her helmet and stacked her bike. Now for the 1.5 km run. "I'm so tired, Mummy!" wailed Milly as she ran past me.

"Just do your best, darling," I yelled to her. I didn't know how she was going to finish it. The next minute, I saw Josiah sprint after her. My darling son ran beside her the whole way, encouraging her to keep going.

We cheered and clapped as they crossed the finish line. Milly was all smiles when Hamish Carter, the Olympian triathlete, presented her with her medal. I glanced over at Josiah. He was grinning with pleasure, too.

Milly and Josiah

Something To Do

- Discuss with your children what an allegory is. Have them look the word up in several dictionaries. The Collins Dictionary's definition of allegory is: 'a symbolic story or poem with a moral.' Ask them to think of different truths this particular allegory portrays. (Life is a journey; our Christian walk is also a journey; there is danger when we wander from God's given path; we have an enemy of our souls who wants to lock us up in a fortress of despair and fear; we have the power of life and death in our tongue - Hopeful was able to warn his brother and exhort him to think differently; we each carry within us a key that will unlock any prison - God's faithful promises etc)

- Ask your children if they can think of any other allegories. Jesus spoke in many parables. Can your children think of any? (The sower and the seed; the vine growers.)

- Do a project together on the life of John Bunyan. He wrote Pilgrim's Progress while he was serving a twelve-year prison term for preaching the gospel.

- Get your children to draw a picture of Hopeful and Christian in prison, and Giant Despair. (I have a wonderful old book of Pilgrim's Progress with amazing pen and ink sketches, drawn by three brothers. I used to love copying them.)

- Get each of your younger children to design and make a key of promise. They might like to choose a special verse they can write on it. Get them to wear it around their necks for a while, and as situations arise, ask them how the key might help to open a lock. For example: the key of promise can open the door of anger. At that time it may glow with a message of forgiveness.

The Gift of Values

- ❖ Think together about who needs encouraging. Make a list. (The tired, the weak, the sad and depressed, the grieving, the fearful, the hopeless and despairing.) Then list together ways you could encourage them. Sometimes all a person needs to hear is, "You can do it!" Some other encouraging phrases: Jesus loves you! I believe in you! The story's not over yet! God is faithful!

Boom Clip

Kate cooked a delicious blueberry and apple pie for dessert tonight. After he'd had his third helping, Sam told her, "Thanks for the pie, Kate. It was so yummy! You should make these pies and sell them on the streets!"

Boom Clip

We had visitors for dinner and I had cooked a large leg of lamb. After she'd finished her meal, Milly took her plate out to the kitchen and then came to thank me for the meal. "Thanks for the dinner, Mummy," she said in a sweet voice. "It was lovely, but the gravy was disgusting." Oh, we laughed at that. She didn't even realize what she'd said wrong. Still, I guess we're half-way there!

So Said...

- ❖ "If someone listens, or stretches out a hand, or whispers a word of encouragement, or attempts to understand, extraordinary things happen." *Loretta Girzartis*
- ❖ "Taking an interest in what others are thinking and doing is often a much more powerful form of encouragement than praise." *Robert Martin*

❖ "There is nothing better than the encouragement of a good friend." *Katherine Butler Hathaway*

❖ "Encouragement is oxygen to the soul." *George M. Adams*

❖ "The spirited horse, which will try to win the race of its own accord, will run even faster if encouraged." *Ovid*

❖ "You don't have to accept the invitation to get angry. Instead, practice forgiveness, empathy and encouragement." *Dan Fallon*

Boom Clip

Samuel came into the room with a frustrated look on his face. "I just can't do it, Mum!" he wailed and tossed the folded origami paper on the desk.

Over the years, Sam's grandpa has taught him how to make all sorts of fantastic things with origami - jumping frogs, boats, birds and turtles. I'd recently found a great book in the library on how to make origami dinosaurs and Samuel had spent the last hour wrestling with a brontosaurus.

Now one of the peculiar things about teachable moments is that they often come at the most inopportune times. It's usually when you're busy, or tired, and not thinking at all about teaching values to your children. I certainly wasn't in the frame of mind to be messing about with an obstinate brontosaurus.

However, just as I opened my mouth to say, "Never mind, Sam. Don't worry about it," I recognized the moment for what it was. I needed to teach Sam how to persevere. That meant putting aside my own agenda for a while and helping Sam work it out. I never find it easy to stop doing something I'm engrossed in, but I am so glad that I did! The look on his face was worth every moment it had cost me. He was so proud of his brontosaurus. He'd kept trying and he'd done it! It was a very important life lesson in perseverance - and for me a lesson in the power of encouragement.

The Gift of Values

I discovered a new formula that day:
I Can't + Encouragement and Perseverance = I Can!

Words To Live By

- "For the despairing man there should be kindness from his friends." *Job 6:14 NASB*

- "We who are strong ought to bear with the failings of the weak and not to please ourselves." *Romans 15:1 NIV*

- "But encourage one another daily, as long as it is called Today, so that none of you may be hardened by sin's deceitfulness." *Hebrews 3:13 NIV*

- "And we urge you, brothers, warn those who are idle, encourage the timid, help the weak, be patient with everyone." *1 Thessalonians 5:14 NIV*

- "For everything that was written in the past was written to teach us, so that through endurance and the encouragement of the Scriptures we might have hope." *Romans 15:4 NIV*

- "Encourage the timid, help the weak, be patient with everyone." *1 Thessalonians 5:14 NIV*

Boom Clip

During my nursing training, I boarded with a beautiful couple who were like parents to me. Mr. Ed, as I called him, was such an encourager. When I went through a really dark time in my life, and felt like everything had gone wrong, he would remind me again and again, "Don't worry, Rose! The story's not over yet!"

That became my catch phrase for many years. When all looked bleak, it helped me remember that God was still writing my life story. And that He had some wonderful chapters ahead.

Dig Deeper

- Read *Pilgrim's Progress*. There are adapted versions of this wonderful book for all ages. It is also available on DVD.

- Watch the DVD *Pollyanna* with your younger children. It is the touching story of a young girl who transforms the loneliness and bitterness of many people's lives through her optimism and encouragement.

- If you are happy to navigate the 'dark' parts of *The Lord of the Rings,* you will discover countless examples of the power of encouragement. Samwise Gamgee is my hero in the story, with his unswerving loyalty to his friend, and his constant encouragement. "You can do it, Master Frodo."

- Get your older children to research in the Bible about Barnabas, *'the son of encouragement.'*

- Watch *The Secret Garden* with your younger children. Both Mary and Colin have to learn to control their tongues. In the end, it is the constant encouragement from Mary and Dicken that helps Colin to walk again. (We preferred the old BBC production, which dealt with the 'magic' episode in quite a different way than the modern film.)

The Gift of Values

The Two Frogs

One hot summer's day, as a group of frogs made their way through the woods, two of them fell into a deep pit. All the other frogs gathered around the pit and gazed down at their friends. The two frogs began to jump frantically. When the others saw how deep the pit was, they began shouting to their friends, "You'll never make it out! It's too deep!"

The two frogs ignored the comments and kept trying to jump up out of the pit with all their might. Their futile efforts distressed the other frogs. They kept telling them to stop; that they were as good as dead. Finally, one of the frogs took heed to what the other frogs were saying and gave up. He fell down and died.

The other frog continued to jump as hard as he could. Once again, the crowd of frogs yelled at him, "Give up! Stop trying! You'll never make it!"

But the frog jumped even harder and finally made it out.

The frogs crowded around him as he lay gasping on the ground. "Didn't you hear us?" they asked.

"Eh, what's that?" asked the frog.

"Didn't you hear us?" they shouted even louder.

"Sorry," said the frog. "I can't hear very well. But thanks for encouraging me the whole time! I would never have made it out without your help."

Think About It

- ❖ Why did the first frog give up?
- ❖ Why did the second frog *not* give up?
- ❖ Ask the children what they think *Proverbs 18:21* means.
- ❖ *Whose* tongue holds the power of death? (Our own!)
- ❖ *Whose* tongue holds the power of life? (Our own!)

Boom Clip

The other day I was talking to the children about words of affirmation and encouragement. I told them that today we would only speak affirming words - quick as a flash, Josiah said, "I'm staying in my room!"

Something To Do

- ❖ Lessons from geese. We had fun doing this one morning. First I read to the children the following facts about geese, and then asked them to think of how it applied to us as a family.

- ❖ Fact 1. As each goose flaps its wings it creates uplift for the bird that follows. By flying in a V formation, the whole flock of geese adds 71% greater flying range than if each bird flew alone. (We help each other when we fly together. We'll get to where we want to go faster and easier, if we stay connected to each other.)

- ❖ Fact 2. When a goose falls out of formation, it suddenly feels the drag and resistance of flying alone. It quickly moves back into formation to take advantage of the lifting power of the bird in front of it. (If we have as much sense as a goose, we'll stay in formation with those headed where we want to go. We must be willing to accept help from others and also give help to others.)

- ❖ Fact 3. When the head goose gets tired, he drops back in the formation and another goose takes his turn at the lead. (No, this doesn't mean that a child can take over the leadership of the family and make the decisions. But it does mean we should all take turns doing the hard work.)

- ❖ Fact 4. Geese flying in formation honk constantly to encourage those in front to keep up speed. (Here is the power of encouragement! We need to speak words of encouragement constantly. Don't fly in silence. Let the others know you appreciate them and love them.)

The Gift of Values

- ❖ **Fact 5.** When a goose gets sick, wounded or shot down, two geese drop out of formation and follow it down to the ground to help it and protect it. They stay with it until it dies or becomes well enough to fly again. Then they fly off with another formation or catch up with the flock. (We are committed to each other! We will stand by each other in the difficult times as well as when we are strong.)

Then I got my little goslings to act out what they'd just learned. We had a lot of fun flying in formation, flapping our wings, honking furiously and taking turns at being in the front of the formation. (This is one of the benefits of being a big family!) When one of the 'geese' fell to the ground, two of the others broke formation and protected it. It made a real racket, but none of us will forget it in a hurry!

- ❖ Make a goose mobile and hang it from the ceiling. We wrote on ours, 'Don't forget to honk!'

- ❖ Work out a family cheerleading chant. The effect of cheerleading is to give encouragement to the team. We've just finished reading *The Children Who Lived in a Barn* by Eleanor Graham. It's about the Dunnet children who go and live together in a barn when their parents disappear for six months after a plane crash. Their family motto was "Up the Dunnets!" which reminded them not to let anyone or anything hold them down.

So Said...

- ❖ "Correction does much, but encouragement does more."
  Johann Wolfgang von Goethe

- ❖ "A word of encouragement during a failure is worth more than an hour of praise after success." *Anon*

- ❖ "One word or a pleasing smile is often enough to raise up a saddened and wounded soul." *Therese of Lisieux*

❖ "You never know when a moment and a few sincere words can have an impact on a life." *Zig Ziglar*

❖ "One of the best parts of being a family is that you can encourage one another. You can put courage into one another. You can believe in one another. You can affirm one another." *Stephen R. Covey*

Words To Live By

❖ "Death and life are in the power of the tongue." *Proverbs 18:21 NIV*

❖ "We have different gifts, according to the grace given us… if it is encouraging, let him encourage." *Romans 12:6-8 NIV*

❖ "Preach the Word; be prepared in season and out of season; correct, rebuke and encourage - with great patience and careful instruction." *2 Timothy 4:2 NIV*

❖ "Encourage and rebuke with all authority. Do not let anyone despise you." *Titus 2:15 NIV*

❖ "But the men of Israel encouraged one another and took up their positions where they had stationed themselves the first day." *Judges 20:22 NIV*

❖ "He… encouraged them with these words; 'Be strong and courageous. Do not be afraid or discouraged because of the king of Assyria and the vast army with him, for there is a greater power with us than with him. With him is only the arm of flesh, but with us is the Lord our God to help us and fight our battles." And the people gained confidence from what Hezekiah the king of Judah said." *2 Chronicles 32:7-9 NIV*

❖ "For you know that we dealt with each of you as a father deals with his own children, encouraging, comforting and urging you to live lives worthy of God, who calls us into his kingdom and glory." *1 Thessalonians 2:11,12 NIV*

The Gift of Values

- "Therefore encourage one another and build each other up, just as in fact you are doing." *1 Thessalonians 5:11 NIV*

- "Do not let any unwholesome talk come out of your mouths, but only what is helpful for building others up according to their needs, that it may benefit those who listen." *Ephesians 4:29 NIV*

- "Let us not give up meeting together, as some are in the habit of doing, but let us encourage one another - and all the more as you see the Day approaching." *Hebrews 10:25 NIV*

- "There is one that speaks rashly like the thrusts of a sword, but the tongue of the wise brings healing." *Proverbs 12:18 NIV*

- "Pleasant words are a honeycomb, sweet to the soul and healing to the bones." *Proverbs 16:24 NIV*

- "A word aptly spoken is like apples of gold in settings of silver." *Proverbs 25:11 NIV*

Boom Clip

It had been a really busy day in the Boom household. Sports, visitors, work around the home. All day, Chris had been feeling under par, and was dreading having to go out at night to do a concert. I, on the other hand, was raring to go, and felt upset that he was so negative about singing that night. Finally, I said to him, "Don't worry about it! I'll do the concert myself!" Mind you, I never expected him to take me up on the offer.

To my amazement Chris said, "Will you? Great!" And that was that. As I packed the car, I became more and more depressed. Why was he *always* so reluctant to sing? Perhaps I was fated to be doing all our concerts on my own from now on. I began to feel more and more sorry for myself. Then seven-year-old Eliza came to me and said in a sweet voice, "Mummy, I'll come with you, if you like."

And so it was, she and I set off together, with me still feeling full of self-pity, even though I knew deep down I was making a mountain out of a molehill.

Ellie sat quietly in the car for the first twenty minutes, scribbling on a piece of paper. When we stopped to get some petrol, she handed it to me. It read:

"To dear Mummy,
If Dad stops singing, you keep going and I'll always be by your side. I will always love you, go with you, sing with you, pray for you, and miss you. And you will always be my mum. You are the best mum in the world. Love from your Eliza."

There were lots of words scribbled out and spelling mistakes, but it was the most precious note she'd ever given me. I cried as I read it over and over, and let go my self-pity. That night my little encourager and I had the most wonderful time together at the concert.

I still have the note in my Bible, and read it with a smile again just this week. Eliza and I are heading to Colorado Springs to do some singing together next month. We can't wait.

Dig Deeper

❖ Watch the DVD *Fly Away Home* with your older children. Wonderful footage of geese flying, and some good examples of the power of encouragement, too.

❖ A great DVD to watch with your older teenagers is *Apollo 13*, which tells of the ill-fated lunar mission of April 1970. When the ground crew try to bring the men safely back to earth, things look near nigh impossible. One of the crew says, "This will be the worst disaster NASA has ever experienced." The flight director replies, "With all due respect, sir, I believe this is going to be our finest hour." He then goes on to tell his

The Gift of Values

team, "Failure is not an option." Gripping watching. A caution though - it does contain a number of profanities. Shame.

- ❖ Read about the twelve spies who were sent out by Moses to explore the land of Canaan. (*Numbers chapters 13 and 14*) Ten spies bring back a negative report. Only Joshua and Caleb encourage the Israelites to believe God and go in to take the land.

- ❖ Research the inspiring story of Wilma Rudolph. The doctors told her that she would never walk. But her mother told her she would. So... she believed her mother!

Despite the polio that had left her crippled, and in the face of all the doctors' damning assessments, Wilma chose to turn her back on all the negative reports. She chose to believe that she could walk again. And she did! She went on to run faster than any woman ever had before: 11 seconds in the 100-metre event at the 1960 Olympics. Wilma Rudolph became the first woman to ever win three gold medals at one Olympics. Her life was an inspiring example of never giving up; of not listening to the voices of doubt; of not being afraid to attempt.

ೋ

Encouragement

In the Camp of Death

The true story of Josef Korbel, imprisoned for his faith in Czechoslovakia.

"Josef Korbel." The thin voice seemed to echo in the courtroom. Josef stood to his feet. He was ready to give his defence against the charges laid against him.

He cleared his throat, and then spoke in a clear voice. "I am standing here for proclaiming the Gospel of Jesus Christ, who died for the sins of the world on the cross of Calvary, to -"

"Enough!" shouted the chairman of the court. Turning to the judge, he said hatefully, "This man deserves the maximum punishment because he was a Salvation Army officer, a religious radical who opposed our Communist regime."

Josef stood in silence as the judge consulted with the committee. *Lord, my life is in Your hands.*

When the judge finally spoke, his voice sounded distant and strange. "Josef Korbel. You are judged by paragraph one for high treason and sentenced to twelve years in prison."

Joseph shook his head as if trying to make sense of it. Then slowly the truth of it sank in. He was going back to prison for twelve more years.

As the prisoners were led from the courtroom, Josef's eyes searched the crowd desperately. At last he saw them. His youngest son, Victor, was leaning his blond head on his brother's shoulder. Helmuth stood straight and tall, with his arm slung protectively around the little boy's shoulders.

A painful lump formed in Josef's throat. Tears sprang to his eyes. *God, look after my boys.*

"Hurry up! Get in!" shouted the guards as they pushed the prisoners into the windowless van.

When the van finally stopped outside the prison gates, Josef stumbled out with the other prisoners and squinted in the bright light. Soldiers yelled at them in harsh voices as they fell in line and began to make their way

The Gift of Values

through the gate. Then Josef heard a sound that stopped him in his tracks. Someone was whistling on the street outside the gate. He knew that tune! It was the familiar song of the Salvation Army. *"Shine brightly for Jesus..."* Joy burst into Josef's heart. Then he listened again. It was Helmuth! His boy must have jumped on his bicycle and followed the van to the prison.

"God go with you, my son!" cried Josef, as a guard roughly pushed him in the back.

Two days later, Josef was transported to the labour camp which had earned the name, The Camp of Death. Josef felt the darkness threaten to swallow him up. *Shine brightly for Jesus...* Again Helmuth's song filled his heart. "Father," prayed Josef, "darkness abounds here. So, let me be Your light."

Helmuth's whistled song was to be a great source of encouragement to Josef in the following years. When the darkness of the prison tried to overwhelm him, Josef sang. He sang every song he could remember, over and over again. Often he closed his eyes and pictured Paul and Silas lying shackled together in a dark, dank prison, singing at the top of their voices.

At night, in the loneliness of his solitary cell, the word of God comforted him. It had been months since he'd given away his New Testament to another prisoner. His wife had managed to smuggle the precious gift to him inside a sandwich. It hadn't been easy to give it away, but he knew the other prisoner desperately needed it. But Josef was not left without the Word of life! All the passages he had ever memorised were written in his heart. Josef paced up and down his cell, speaking them out loud. "Blessed is the man who does not walk in the counsel of the wicked or stand in the way of sinners or sit in the seat of mockers. But his delight is in the law of the Lord, and on his word he meditates day and night. He is like a tree planted by the streams of water, which yields its fruit in season and whose leaf does not wither... for the Lord watches over the way of the righteous, but the way of the wicked will perish."

Josef lifted his heart in thanksgiving. "Thank You, God," he prayed. "You are watching over me! Help me to shine brightly for You in this dark place. Let me be like a tree planted by the waters, with leaves that are ever green!"

Encouragement

Josef Korbel was released on the 2nd of September, 1959, after serving ten years of his sentence. Ten long years since hearing his son whistle to him as he entered the prison. Ten years with no-one to encourage him to stay strong and keep faith. But during those long years, Josef had learned the wonderful secret of encouraging his own heart. When the iron gates of Leopoldov fortress swung open, Josef stood for a moment, blinking in the bright sunshine. A feeling of deep insecurity and confusion swept over him. What should he do? Where should he go? For ten years he had been watched constantly by armed guards. Now there was no-one to tell him what to do. Josef stared at the open fields that lay ahead of him. No, not there. They were too open, too wide. He glanced to his left and saw a dark forest. The trees' welcome shadows seemed to offer him the protection and shelter he longed for. Like a hunted animal he ran towards the forest and flung himself on the grass beneath the mighty fir trees. His heart pounded with a strange mixture of fear and inexpressible joy. For a long time he lay on his back, weeping. Slowly the incredible truth began to sink in. He was free. Free to go home. He pressed a broken twig to his cheeks and drank in the smell of pine. "Father," he cried in a wordless prayer. "You are faithful."

Josef Korbel was reunited with his family and continued to share with other Czechs about Jesus. Helmuth was himself imprisoned for two and a half years for preaching the Gospel. Victor was later forced to serve in the Communist controlled Czech Army. He was eventually killed by the Communists for witnessing about Jesus. As the persecution in Czechoslovakia intensified, the Korbel family made the decision to escape one at a time, so as not to arouse suspicion. They were reunited in America, where Josef continued to speak with others about God's wonderful love and protecting power, and to share with Christians about the needs of their persecuted brothers and sisters behind the Iron Curtain.

Think About It

- Why was Josef imprisoned?

- What did Helmuth do that encouraged his father so much?

- Ask the children if they can think of other seemingly small things we can do, that may be a huge encouragement to others.

- How had his wife managed to get him a Bible?

- How did Josef encourage himself during the long years of imprisonment?

- What *was* the Iron Curtain?

- What can we do to encourage our own hearts?

Boom Clip

I smiled to myself as I listened to Jacob practise his new piano piece over and over again in the other room. Big sister Kate has proved to be a wonderful teacher, and Jacob a very keen student. He finished the song with a flourish and then I heard him clap his little hands vigorously and say, "Bravo! Bravo!"

When I entered the room, smiling at his enthusiastic applause, he looked at me with a slightly bashful look and explained, "There was no one here to encourage me, Mum, so I did it myself!"

Something To Do

- Find Czechoslovakia on a map. Get your children to research about the division of the country in 1993 into Slovakia and The Czech Republic.

- When Corrie ten Boom and her nephew were arrested by the Gestapo, they both had portions of Scripture written on paper and hidden in their shoes. Corrie had written out *Romans 8*. The Gestapo eventually found the pieces of paper, but it was a great comfort to Corrie to know they could never take the Word of God from her - she had also hidden it in her heart. She never realized how important those memory verses would be to her until one night in the concentration camp. Corrie heard that many women were being taken to the gas chambers. She hid behind a fence and whispered words of encouragement and scripture to every single woman that walked past.

Get each of your children to choose a verse and write it on a piece of paper. Then tell them to hide it in their shoe. Have some fun discovering which verse each of you has chosen.

❖ Choose a passage of Scripture and memorise it together. Doing this regularly will be a huge blessing to you and your children. You'll be amazed how easily your young children will take to it. Start small, but do it often. When I was in my twenties, I started memorising the book of James. My dad was astonished. "How can you possibly memorise a whole book?" he asked. "Just verse by verse, Dad," I told him. "And you'll find it gets easier and easier!" Well, he took me at my word and went on to memorize larger and larger portions of the Bible. Now, at age eighty-five, he knows many books by heart. I am the one to be astonished now! Dad tells me that having the Word of God hidden in his heart is one of the greatest blessings of his life.

❖ Sing together some rousing praise choruses or hymns! To make it something the children will remember, try tying some of them up together and have them pretend they're in prison, like Paul and Silas. Or better yet, you could act out the whole story of *Acts 16:12 - 35*. What a fantastic story!

❖ Get your older children to research the Iron Curtain.

❖ Research the work of Amnesty International.

❖ *Voice of the Martyrs* magazine is a wonderful resource that also includes articles specifically aimed at children. Your children will be able to learn facts about the suffering church, pray for those in restricted nations and learn how they can help.

Boom Clip

When we returned as a family to New Zealand in 1966, after three years in Papua New Guinea, my mother never dreamed it would be a permanent move. For many years she yearned to be back on the mission field. But God had other plans...

Years ago, when Mum was just 26, she used to dream about becoming a famous writer. Then one day, the Lord spoke very clearly to her.

"Someday you will write a lot. But it will be for My glory, not yours."

Mum was thrilled. Perhaps she would write a great book that would bless and inspire thousands of people? Or maybe a novel that would draw people close to God?

God's *'someday'* arrived one evening when Mum was listening to a message on cassette by Joy Dawson. Joy said to her audience, "God wants to encourage someone here tonight who has a letter-writing ministry. Over the years you have written many letters, and people have replied saying how they were so blessed by what you had written. The Lord wants you to take this ministry of letter writing more seriously, for the ministry He has given you is to encourage His people."

Joy's words burned into Mum's heart. Letter writing! Not exactly the wonderful writing ministry my mother had envisaged. But she couldn't shake the words from her mind. Several weeks later, her pastor asked if she would be willing to write to the church's missionaries. So it began.

Over the next few years Mum wrote to everyone the Lord brought across her path - the sick, the depressed, the hurting, and a growing number of missionaries.

Many of these people continued to receive her letters regularly over a long period of time.

Mum could talk for hours about all the people she has 'met' through her letters. One of my favourite stories is about a Jewish *'refusenik'* man imprisoned in Siberia. The *refuseniks* were Russian Jews who were forbidden to emigrate to Israel, and were often imprisoned for the crime of wanting to leave the motherland. Mum had been given a list of *refuseniks* in Siberia by Amnesty International. Her letter of encouragement to Vladimir arrived the day after he'd had a dream of a white woman offering him bread. Vladimir was only allowed to write one letter to his wife every couple of months. In his next letter he included Mum's address and asked his wife to write to her and give her a message - *Genesis 40:14*.

When Mum looked up the scripture reference, she heard the cry of one man's heart far away in Siberia - *"Please show kindness to me; make mention of me to Pharaoh and get me out of this prison."*

Mum immediately wrote a letter to Amnesty International, telling them of the contact Vladimir had made with her. There was great excitement at her news, as they had presumed he was dead. They promised Mum they would do their very best to get him released and reunited with his wife.

When Mum first began writing letters, she always included a scripture at the top, and decorated it with a simple drawing of flowers and bees. People wrote back saying they couldn't bear to throw the letters away. So Mum decided to include a handcrafted bookmark in each of her letters.

She asked each missionary to translate encouraging verses into the language of the people group they were working with. Then Mum sent the missionaries as many bookmarks as they needed to give away.

From humble beginnings this ministry has grown and developed in an amazing way. Now, Mum sends out thousands of bookmarks all around the world, in over 65 languages - Turkish, Norwegian, Russian, Hebrew, Hungarian, and Ukrainian, to name a few. They have been used in hospitals, prisons, ports, refugee camps and outreaches.

The Gift of Values

I had a call a few years ago from a family friend who is involved in prison ministry. He told me that during a recent visit to the medium security prison, an inmate had turned to a place in his Bible which was marked with one of Mum's distinctive bookmarks. When my friend saw it, he excitedly told the inmate, "I know the lady who made this bookmark!"

The prisoner told my friend that he had never met my mother. She had heard about him through one of his relatives, and had written to share with him about the Lord. The love and concern in her letter had deeply touched him and he had cherished the bookmark ever since.

If anyone asks Mum what she feels is her 'calling', she doesn't hesitate. "God has called me to be an encourager."

Well, the time finally came in 2002, when the 'encourager' needed to avail herself of modern technology - email! So for her eightieth birthday, we bought her a computer. And my computer illiterate mum put her fears aside and learned to use it! Now her words of encouragement fly out across the world at lightning speed.

It's been over thirty years since we returned from New Guinea, and Mum has never been back to the mission field. But each morning, she prays at her desk and asks the Lord for the words to write. And God opens a window from her small study into dozens of countries around the world.

What an inspiration she is to me! I wrote the following poem for her on her eightieth birthday.

The Encourager

When a soul burns with passion
The heart soon overflows;
And when pen is put to paper
The miracle of encouragement grows.

For from the depths of wisdom
And life's experience flows
A boundless river of blessing
To a multitude of thirsty souls.

For 'tis not merely words
That take themselves to flight
When you sit before your desk
And ask for the words to write.

But as your prayers take form in ink
And encouragement is penned,
The power of heaven is loosed on earth
And Christ's love revealed to men.

So Said...

- ❖ "I believe in the sun even when it is not shining. I believe in love even when not feeling it. I believe in God even when He is silent." *Anonymous Jewish inscription in a cellar hideout in Germany.*

- ❖ "Chop your own wood and it will warm you twice." *Henry Ford* (I love this one! It is so applicable in this chapter. We must learn how to feed the 'fire of our faith' ourselves and not just rely on other people to throw on the wood.)

- ❖ "We cannot presume there will always be someone beside us to encourage us when we are weak or afraid. We must learn how to be our own encouragers." *R J. Boom*

The Gift of Values

- "Someone asked me recently why I always speak about the need for Bibles even after I've delivered so many to a particular area. The answer is simple… the more Bibles we bring to restricted countries, the more Bibles they want because of the tremendous amount of encouragement it brings." *Brother Andrew*

- "Too often we underestimate the power of a touch, a smile, a kind word, a listening ear, an honest compliment, or the smallest act of caring, all of which have the potential to turn a life around.' *Leo Buscaglia*

- "A friend is someone who knows the song in your heart and sings it back to you when you have forgotten how it goes." *Anon*

Words To Live By

- "Why are you downcast, O my soul? Why so disturbed within me? Put your hope in God, for I will yet praise him, my Saviour and my God." *Psalm 42:11 NIV*

- "If your law had not been my delight, I would have perished in my affliction. I will never forget your precepts, for by them you have preserved my life." *Psalm 119:92 NIV* (This verse is my testimony! It was God's word that helped me through the dark days of testing and trial when I was in my twenties.)

- "My soul is weary with sorrow; strengthen me according to your word." *Psalm 119:28 NIV*

- "Great peace have they who love your law, and nothing can make them stumble." *Psalm 119:165 NIV*

- "For whatever was written in earlier times was written for our instruction, that through perseverance and the encouragement of the Scriptures we might have hope." *Romans 15:4 NASB*

Encouragement

- "But you, beloved, building yourselves up on your most holy faith; praying in the Holy Spirit; keep yourselves in the love of God, waiting anxiously for the mercy of our Lord Jesus Christ to eternal life." *Jude v20, 21 NASB*

- "Who shall separate us from the love of Christ? Shall trouble or hardship or persecution or famine or nakedness or danger or sword? As it is written: 'For your sake we face death all day long; we are considered as sheep to be slaughtered.' No, in all these things we are more than conquerors through him who loved us. For I am convinced that neither death nor life, neither angels nor demons, neither the present nor the future, nor any powers, neither height nor depth, nor anything else in all creation, will be able to separate us from the love of God that is in Christ Jesus our Lord." *Romans 8:35 - 39 NIV* (What triumphant words! I remember seeing the fear in my children's faces on the day the twin towers fell in New York. I felt prompted by the Lord to talk with them about this wonderful passage and memorize it together. Jacob was only three at the time, so we decided to make up a song from these verses. It's amazing how easy it is to memorize Scripture when it's in a song! I encourage any of you who have the slightest bit of musical talent to write songs with your children. You may never perform it for others, but the Word of God will be hidden in your hearts.)

- "Remember the Lord's people who are in jail and be concerned for them. Don't forget those who are suffering, but imagine that you are there with them." *Hebrews 13:3 CEV*

- "After they had been severely flogged, they were thrown into prison, and the jailor was commanded to guard them carefully. Upon receiving such orders, he put them in the inner cell and fastened their feet in stocks. About midnight Paul and Silas were praying and singing hymns to God and the other prisoners were listening to them." *Acts 16:23-25 NIV*

Dig Deeper

- Read the inspiring story of Brother Andrew in *God's Smuggler*. God spoke to this young Dutch missionary with the words, "Strengthen what remains and is on the point of death." (*Revelation 3:2*) From that day in 1955, Brother Andrew believed that no doors could be closed. No borders, no barriers, no armies could withstand the power of prayer… and no power on earth could ever chain God's Word. With this confidence he smuggled in countless Bibles to closed countries and encouraged the persecuted believers behind the Iron Curtain.

- Read together the passage in *1 Samuel chapter 30* that gives the account of David returning from war to find his city of Ziklag burnt and plundered. Not a soul was left in the city; all had been captured. The men spoke of stoning David in their bitterness and grief, but David encouraged himself in the Lord and went on to take everything back in a great victory. Discuss what may have happened if he hadn't strengthened his heart.

- Read more of Josef Korbel's testimony in his book *In My Enemy's Camp*, written with Frank Allnut.

- Read *The Viking Series* by Lois Walfrid Johnson. When Briana O'Toole is taken captive by the Vikings, her brother, Devin, is no longer there to encourage her. But she remembers the secret sign they made up to encourage each other without words - the sign that meant 'Courage to win.' Briana learns how to stand strong on her own and be a light for Jesus in a strange and foreign land. A great read-aloud series for a winter's night!

- A wonderful book for your teenagers to read is *Jesus Freaks* by dc Talk and *The Voice of the Martyrs*. In the back of the book are some practical ways to help the persecuted church.

- Visit *The Voice of the Martyrs* website: *www.persecution.com* and sign up for their monthly newsletter. Prayer requests and updates are available on the website.

Value Three

SELF CONTROL

The biggest truth about this value is displayed right there in its name - self-control. We can't be constant monitors and controllers for our children. They need to learn to control their appetites, emotions and actions themselves. It is their ultimate responsibility. You'll probably find, as I have, that each child will wrestle with his or her own area of temptation. For one it might be the struggle to moderate what they eat, for another it might be their quick and ready temper. And for yet another, it might be the challenge of restricting their time spent on the computer. More of that later.

The worrying, slightly scary thing about all the values in this book is that we, as parents, are expected to demonstrate them to our children. We are the ones who should model them to our families and so teach them by example. In fact, I hope and pray that this book will be as much for the benefit and spiritual growth of the adult readers, as it is for them to use as a resource and tool with their children.

In this chapter I want to highlight the need for our children to develop self-control in three specific areas - their words, their appetites and their tempers. However, there are many other areas where we all need to develop self-control. The wonderful and encouraging thing is that we *can* develop it. Self-control is one of the fruits of the Spirit as listed in Galatians 5:22, 23. And like the other eight fruits, it grows in our lives as we seek to live by the Spirit.

The Gift of Values

One of the stories in this chapter will introduce your children to Dr. Ben Carson, the famed neurosurgeon. The fact that he ever became who he is today is a tremendous story of hope: a testament to the fact that we can change.

Be open to the possibility of seeing areas in your own life as you work through this chapter. I remember hearing a preacher say that throughout our whole lives we should always be students and teachers. What an amazing and exciting truth. We should never stop learning. And we should never stop sharing with others what we have discovered.

༄

Waldo Pigginson

nce upon a time there was a small boy named Waldo Pigginson. He was a nice looking boy, with curly blonde hair and mischievous green eyes. But he was not exactly a nice little boy. In fact, many people considered Waldo Pigginson to be a first-class brat.

There were three things that Waldo was very good at:
1. Hiding
2. Running away
3. Shrugging his shoulders

And there were two words he was very fond of using. Now, you might hope they were, 'Thank you,' or 'Excuse me,' or 'I'm sorry.' But they were not.

"Waldo Pigginson! Your room is a pigsty!" said Mum one morning.

Waldo shrugged his shoulders. "Who cares?" he said as he ran out the door and down the path to catch the bus for school.

At playtime, Waldo pushed his way to the front of the line for the slide.

"Stop it!" said Margery Thimble, who was only six but had a lot of pluck. "You shouldn't push."

"Who cares!" sneered Waldo as he shrugged his shoulders and climbed the slide.

Dinnertime was always stressful in the Pigginson family. Try as they might, Waldo's parents could not get him to eat any vegetables. Nor would he eat any fruit. But he had no problem at all in consuming vast amounts of potatoe chips, ice cream and sweets.

"Waldo Pigginson!" said his mother in frustration. "Soon enough your teeth will be rotten."

But Waldo just shrugged his shoulders and said a garbled something that was difficult to make out with a mouth full of sweets. But to his parents it sounded suspiciously like his two favourite words.

Whenever it came time for chores, Waldo was nowhere to be found.

The Gift of Values

"Waldo," called Dad. "Where are you?"

Waldo sniggered from his hideout in the middle of the thick pittosporum hedge.

"Waldo! Come and fetch the firewood!"

Waldo crouched very still and put a hand over his mouth to muffle his laughter.

"Waldo Pigginson," called Dad in frustration, "if you don't start doing some work around the place, you'll become a fat, lazy boy!"

He stomped back into the house, which was a shame really, because if he had stayed where he was, he would have heard the hedge snort like a pig, and whisper, 'Who cares!'

But things finally caught up with young Waldo Pigginson. It began on the day of the school picnic.

"Waldo Pigginson, your hair is an absolute mess!" said Mum as they sat down for lunch. "It looks like a bird's nest!"

Waldo grinned and shrugged his shoulders. "Who cares!" he said.

Now it just so happened that at the very same instant that Waldo's two favourite words left his mouth, a swallow flew overhead and spotted him.

"Aha!" said she. "The perfect place to lay my eggs!" And she swooped down and landed on Waldo's head.

"Ouch! Yeow!" shouted Waldo, as the bird began to pull at his hair and arrange her nest. "Someone help me! There's a bird in my hair!"

All the children gathered around to see the funny sight. As Waldo's mother made her way over to help her son, she tried to hide a smile, but her laughing eyes betrayed her.

The next day, Waldo woke up very unhappy. He had an aching pain in the right side of his jaw. He gave it a rub and then popped his two-day-old everlasting gob-stopper in his mouth.

"Yeeeeow!" he yelled and leapt out of bed. The gob-stopper fell on the floor and rolled out the door. Waldo chased it down the hall and caught it. He put it back in his mouth.

"Ow!" he yelled again. This time he spat it out with such force it knocked over Mum's prized porcelain jar.

"Waldo!" cried Mum. "What on earth are you doing?"

"It's my tooth!" moaned Waldo. "I'm in agony."

"So," said Mum, "time for the dentist."

It was a sorry-looking Waldo Pigginson who made his way into the dentist's waiting room that day. He sat glowering at the other patients. A freckle-faced girl giggled at him. It was Margery Thimble. Waldo glared at her. Margery leaned over and whispered something to her mother. Waldo inched forward on his seat.

"That's the fat boy who had a bird in…"

Waldo looked behind him. A grey-haired lady sat reading a magazine. His face turned pink. *Fat! How dare that awful little girl call me fat!* But when Waldo glanced down, he saw that the button on his jeans had popped open and a fat roll of tummy showed beneath his shirt. His face turned pinker still.

"Waldo Pigginson, you can come in now," said the dental nurse.

Waldo tried to suck in his tummy as he walked past Margery Thimble into the examination room. He couldn't. But he had more important things to worry about once he lay back in the chair.

"Waldo, no more sweets!" warned the dentist sternly. "You need at least five fillings. And if you carry on eating rubbish, you'll need many more."

Waldo Pigginson made a strange gurgling sound while the dentist kept poking around in his mouth. Now you might guess that what he tried to say was, 'Who cares,' but you would be wrong. Because in actual fact, Waldo Pigginson never said those words again.

Think About It

- What three things was Waldo Pigginson very good at?
- What were his two favourite words?
- When did he run away?
- What happened to him at the school picnic?
- Why did he finally change his ways?

Something To Do

- Play the *Too Much* game with your younger children. Richard and Linda Eyre recommend this game in their book, *Teaching Your Children Values*. First explain to your children the concept of moderation. Then tell them how to play. You say, "Too much…" and they think of something that you shouldn't have too much of. Then they need to say what might happen if you have too much of that thing. For example:

    Too much food….you might get fat.
    Too much TV…you don't play outside.
    Too much tomato sauce…you can't taste your food!
    Too many sweets….you might need fillings.

- Give your older children a clothing allowance. We began this some time ago, and it didn't take the children long to realise that you only get to spend the money once. One of them liked to spend it all at the beginning of the month as soon as she got it. But she soon learned! It was a good lesson in self-control.

- You may like to do a partial fast with your older children. Encourage them to think of something they could do without for a week. It may be sweets, computer time, meat or any number of things. You may like to try a 'Daniel' diet of vegetables and fruit and water. It does us all good to practice self-control.

❖ If you have a computer in your home, you may need to have a family conference and determine what is an acceptable amount of time to spend each day on the computer. This is one area that is a huge challenge for children, especially boys! In many ways, the computer is harder to moderate than TV. At least a TV programme or DVD only lasts a set amount of time. But the computer games can be played for hours on end. We have to somehow teach our children to know how much time is 'too much'.

I have talked to many parents about this, and heard of many varied ways that parents have tackled the challenge.

I think one vital key is making your children 'clock in and clock out.' Get your children to write down each day exactly how much time they've spent on the computer, and then tally it up at the end of the week. They will probably be surprised at just how much time has been swallowed up. In the end, they are going to have to 'own' this challenge themselves. When they leave home, Mum isn't going to be there to say, "Don't you think you've been on there long enough?" They need to realise that excessive time on the computer is costing them in other vital areas of their lives.

I recently read a great article by John Cowan entitled, *'Are You in Charge of your Kids' Media Diet?'* He comments that 'modern media can unite people on different sides of the planet, and yet can separate people in the same room'. Cowan encourages parents to establish a family culture where TV, phones, computers and games are a privilege, rather than a right, and to retain the right to control their child's access to them. He recommends budgeting our children's media consumption by setting a limited number of hours each week, and then helping them to plan how they will spend those media hours. It will train them to be more discerning, rather than just passively soaking up whatever is fired at them.

The Gift of Values

❖ Read about the self-control of King David. He refused to exact revenge on King Saul, even though his men urged him to kill the king as he slept. (*1 Samuel 24*) Another time David exercised self-control and spared Saul's life, even when he was prompted by others to kill him. (*1 Samuel 26*) By contrast, David did not exercise self-control when he saw Bathsheba. (*2 Samuel 11*) Many people suffered because of this lack of self-control.

Boom Clip

Tonight at the dinner table, Josiah baited Emily by taking ages to put what she wanted on the Lazy Susan. Typical big brother stuff. True to form, Emily made some loud, exasperated noises. But she wasn't the only one annoyed. However when I told Joe to stop being so irritating, he replied, "But Mum, I'm helping Milly to develop self-control." Grrr.

So Said...

❖ "The foundation of excellence lies in self-control." *H.L. Baugher*

❖ "There are two things over which you have complete dominion, authority and control - your mind and your mouth." *African proverb*

❖ "Self- discipline begins with the mastery of your thoughts. If you don't control what you think, you can't control what you do. Simply, self-discipline enables you to think first and act afterwards." *Napoleon Hill*

❖ "It's easier to suppress the first desire than to satisfy all that follow." *Anon*

❖ "I am the master of my own fate; I am the captain of my soul." *William Ernest Henley.*

❖ "The exercise of self-control prevents desire from becoming dictator." *Charles Swindoll*

❖ "If a man will understand how intimately, yea, how inseparably, self-control and happiness are associated, he has but to look into his own heart, and upon the world around. Looking upon the lives of men and women, he will perceive how the hasty word, the bitter retort, the act of deception, the blind prejudice and foolish resentment bring wretchedness and even ruin in their train." *James Allen*

❖ "Developing this discipline is a personal matter. We can depend upon no one else to develop our own discipline of self-control. Paul says, 'I box, I run, I discipline my body.' If someone else has to restrain us, it's not self-control." *Charles Swindoll*

❖ "Self determination is fine, but it needs to be tempered with self-control." *Anon*

❖ "Someone has to control you; the best one to do it is you. Control your body and tongue, whatever you have to do" *Anon*

Words To Live By

❖ "But the fruit of the Spirit is love, joy, peace, patience, kindness, goodness, faithfulness, gentleness and self-control." *Galatians 5:22 NIV*

❖ "The end of all things is near. Therefore be clear minded and self-controlled so you can pray." *1 Peter 4:7 NIV*

❖ "Daniel then said to the guard… 'Please test your servants for ten days: Give us nothing but vegetables to eat and water to drink. Then compare our appearance with that of the young men who eat the royal food, and treat your servants in accordance with what you see.' So he agreed to this and tested them for ten days. At the end of ten days they looked healthier and better nourished than any of the young men who ate the royal food. So the guard took away their choice food and the wine they were to drink and gave them vegetables instead." *Daniel 1:11-16 NIV*

Boom Clip

The strains of The Blue Danube wafted through the still night air. Our large front lawn looked magical, all lit up with citronella flares and candles and lamps, and several braziers blazing. It was our midsummer evening Strauss Ball. Sam and Jake both looked wonderful in the black top hats they'd made out of cardboard. Kate, Eliza and Milly all looked beautiful. I had spent several hours curling their long hair into ringlets, and they each wore a beautiful ball gown. Chris looked very handsome in his black tails, complete with lacy cravat (my petticoat).

I went to the gate and began to welcome the first guests who were arriving. Milly came bounding up to greet them with me. I glanced at her and smiled, and then spun around and stared at her again.

Something didn't look right. I peered at her in the darkness. "Milly, what have you done with your hair?" I asked, feeling a familiar sense of dread.

She had the good grace to look embarrassed. "I got sick of the curls falling in my face," she explained. "They were annoying me."

Aaaaagh. I couldn't believe it. My impulsive girl had simply cut off the ringlets at her scalp.

A year later I found the long curls shoved under the bottom of her bookcase.

Dig Deeper

- ❖ Watch *Willie Wonka and the Chocolate Factory*. Augustus Gloop showcases the great need for moderation! We enjoy the old version of the film best.

- ❖ Watch *Walk the Line* with your older children. It tells the story of Johnny Cash and the struggle he had with alcohol and drugs.

- Read *The World of Winnie-the-Pooh* and *The House at Pooh Corner* by A.A. Milne. Pooh gets stuck in Rabbit's front door, and has the audacity to tell Rabbit his door is not big enough. Rabbit tells him sternly, "It all comes of eating too much."

- Enjoy together the wonderful world of *The Wind in the Willows* by Kenneth Grahame. Here are some wonderful characters to teach your children many lessons. Poor old Toad simply cannot control himself. He steals shiny motor cars and ends up in prison. Can his loyal friends reform the incorrigible Toad?

- Read *Where the Red Fern Grows* by Wilson Rawls. It tells the inspiring story of young Billy's longing to own his own pair of coon dogs, and his absolute commitment to work hard and save the money to buy them. This is also available on DVD and made a great night's entertainment for the Booms.

- Read *Just-So Stories* by Rudyard Kipling with your younger children. You will read how Rhinoceros got his skin, which will teach you not to be selfish; how Whale got his throat, which will teach you not to be greedy.

- One of my all time favourite books is *The Christmas Miracle of Jonathan Toomey* by Susan Wojciechowski. Mr Toomey is a woodcarver with a very sad past. One day, the widow McDowell and her son Thomas come to his door to ask him to carve a special nativity scene. Thomas must be very self-controlled and sit very quietly and still if Mr Toomey is going to tolerate him watching him. Once, when he wanted to sneeze, he pressed a finger under his nose to hold it back. Once, when he wanted desperately to scratch his leg, he counted to twenty to keep his mind off the itch. Now, I know the main topic of the story is not really self-control, but it's such a beautiful story, I just had to get it in here somewhere - those of you who haven't discovered this treasure will thank me for it!

The Two Pirates

Sam was invited to spend a couple of days with a friend. He was very excited, but his little brother was equally sad! "Why can't I go, too?" asked Jacob.

I told him it was good for Sam to have some time by himself with his friend. "Would you like to have Aljoh come and stay the night with you?" I asked. His face lit up and he nodded vigorously. Aljoh is Jacob's best friend.

Sam and Jake and Aljoh all played happily together until Sam's friend arrived to pick him up. I saw Jake's lip tremble as Sam waved goodbye from the car. When Aljoh went home to get his pyjamas and toothbrush, I could see that Jacob was still missing his brother. I gave him a hug and said, "Never mind, Jake. Let's go and make your bunk into a pirate ship for tonight. Aljoh will love that."

He cheered up at that and helped me hang sheets all around the bunk.

The phone went about half an hour later. It was Aljoh's mum. She told me that Aljoh was sobbing and very upset. Apparently when Sam's friend arrived to pick him up, Jacob had turned to Aljoh and said, "I wish you weren't coming to my house! I want to go with Sam."

Oh dear. I felt dreadful. I called Jacob into my room and told him there was a very sad little boy up the road. I asked him if he knew why Aljoh was crying. He thought for a minute and then said, "Oh, Mum. That's right. Remember? He hurt his knee on the tramp!"

"No," I said. "That's not why. Think again."

He thought for a few minutes and then shook his head. "Why, Mummy? Why's Aljoh crying?"

"Did you say something that might have upset him, Jacob?" I asked gently.

Slowly understanding dawned on his face. "I didn't mean it, Mummy," he said in a little voice. "I only said it 'cos I was sad Sam was going."

"Maybe. But Aljoh didn't know that. He doesn't want to stay the night anymore."

Self Control

Jake looked at me with a tragic face and then fell into my arms sobbing. He cried for at least a minute and then said in a shaky voice, "But he's my best friend, Mummy."

"I know," I said. "But people get hurt when you say things like that." I let him cry for a while, then said, "Do you want to go and see him and say you're sorry?"

He nodded his head against my chest.

When we walked in their front door, I glanced down at my little son. His lip trembled and his face was still streaked with tears. Aljoh came out to meet him. He was smiling. "I forgive you, Jacob!" he said, before Jacob could say anything. Jacob started to cry again and said in a little voice, "I'm sorry, Aljoh. You're my best friend."

Then the two boys hugged each other.

Two pirates went to bed together that night and I heard them giggling behind the sheets. "Watch out for rats!" I joked as I turned off the light.

The next morning, they found a dead mouse on the carpet, left there by our cat, the great hunter. The two pirates picked it up and carefully put it in Milly's drawer for a surprise.

Think About It

❖ Why did Jacob say such a mean thing to his best friend? (It was a reaction to how he was feeling at the time.)

❖ Get your children to think of some words to describe how Aljoh would have felt. (hurt; let-down; betrayed; unwanted; unloved)

❖ Why do you think Jacob didn't guess straight away why Aljoh was upset? (He had forgotten all about his hasty words. He hadn't meant them, so he didn't realize how deeply it had hurt Aljoh.)

The Gift of Values

❖ How important was it for Jacob to go and see his friend and put things right? (VERY!)

Something To Do

❖ Make a bow and arrow together. Get the children to each have turns loosing an arrow and trying to catch it before it flies away. It's impossible. Tell them that our spoken words can't be retrieved either. Once we speak them out they fly to their target.

❖ Let the children squeeze out some toothpaste. Then get them to try and put it back in the tube. Not so easy!

❖ Read the following short story to your children.

> John Wesley was once approached by a lady who felt terrible about the fact that she'd been gossiping and spreading rumors all around the village. "What can I do to make amends?" she asked.
>
> "You are to pluck a chicken as you walk around the village," he replied after a moment's thought.
>
> The lady did as she was told, and soon returned to Wesley. "Is that all?" she asked.
>
> "No," he replied, looking at her straight in the eye. "Now, you must go around the village and gather up every single feather."

❖ Visit a second hand store and buy a feather pillow. Get your children to cut it open outside on a windy day and shake it in the wind. Then tell them to try and catch all the feathers and put them back in the pillow. It will serve as a good reminder of how impossible it is to retract your words.

❖ Read *James 3:3, 4* together and then get your younger children to try drawing a horse. Make sure they draw the bridle and bit! The boys might like to draw a big ship - make sure they draw in the little rudder!

❖ One of the best things we can teach our children to do is to think before they speak. Get your children to make up an acronym for the word 'think'. They will probably come up with some really good ones.

T - is it Truthful?
H - is it Helpful?
I - is it Inspiring?
N - is it Necessary?
K - is it Kind?

❖ Teach your young children the little Sunday school song *Oh, be careful little eyes, what you see.* Verse two is especially relevant here.

Oh, be careful little eyes, what you see.
Oh, be careful little eyes, what you see.
There's a Father up above, looking down in tender love,
So be careful little eyes, what you see.

Be careful little mouth what you say…
Be careful little ears what you hear…
Be careful little hands, what you touch…
Be careful little feet, where you go…

Boom Clip

This year we bought eleven acres of farm land, complete with lots of native trees and a lovely river for the children to mess around in. I think one of the reasons it hadn't sold earlier was that all over the land lay huge piles of wood and branches from felled macrocarpa trees. However, it's amazing how quickly we cleaned it up with the help of a willing brother-in-law and his expertise with a digger! He rolled the huge logs and piles of rotten timber into five big piles, and then we set them alight. Samuel, my eight-year-old son, begged to be allowed to light one of the piles. And all it took was one small match. He couldn't get over it. He said, "Look at the huge fire, Mummy! And all from that one match!"

The Gift of Values

It was a great opportunity to talk about the formidable power our words have. As it says in the book of James, our words can start a tremendously destructive fire. "Consider what a great forest is set on fire by a small spark. The tongue also is a fire…" (James 3:5, 6)

Those five fires burnt for ten days! A wonderful object lesson about controlling our tongues and measuring the words we speak.

So Said...

- "If you can't say sumpthin' nice, don't say anythin' at all." *Thumper in Bambi*

- "Criticism often takes from the tree both caterpillars and blossoms together." *Anon*

- "Do not discharge in haste the arrow which can never return. It is easy to destroy happiness; most difficult to restore it." *Herder*

- "The art of conversation is not only to say the right thing in the right place, but to leave unsaid the wrong things at the tempting moment." *Lady Dorothy Nevill*

- "Praise where praise is due." *Anon*

- "A still tongue makes a wise head." *Anon*

- "A sharp tongue is the quickest way to cut your own throat." *Anon*

- "If you have something to say, raise your hand… and place it over your mouth!" *Anon*

- "To be truly free is to be in control of my appetites and habits, not to be under their control." *Anon*

- "If you are first a fault to see, be not the first to make it known." *Anon*

- "To do all the talking and not be willing to listen is a form of greed." *Democritus of Abdera, 4th-5th century B. C.*

Self Control

- "To keep love brimming in the loving cup, whenever you're wrong, admit it. Whenever you're right, shut up." *Ogden Nash*

- "The tongue is but three inches long, yet it can kill a man six feet high." *Japanese proverb*

- "In resolving conflict, how you say it is as important as what you say." *Rick Warren*

- "Never miss a good chance to shut up." *Will Rogers*

Words To Live By

- "May the words of my mouth and the meditation of my heart be pleasing in your sight, O Lord, my Rock and my Redeemer." *Psalm 19:14 NIV*

- "There is one that speaks rashly like the thrusts of a sword, but the tongue of the wise brings healing." *Proverbs 12:18 NIV*

- "Without wood, a fire goes out; without gossip, a quarrel dies down. As charcoal to burning embers and as wood to fire, so is a quarrelsome man for kindling strife." *Proverbs 26:20-21 NIV*

- "Death and life are in the power of the tongue." *Proverbs 18:21 NIV*

- "I am in the midst of lions; I lie among ravenous beasts, men whose teeth are spears, whose tongues are sharp swords." *Psalm 57:4 NIV*

- "They make ready their tongue like a bow, to shoot lies;" *Jeremiah 9:3 NIV*

- "If anyone considers himself religious, and yet does not keep a tight rein on his tongue, he deceives himself and his religion is worthless." *James 1:26 NIV*

- "When we put bits into the mouths of horses to make them obey us, we can turn the whole animal. Or take ships as an example. Although they are so large and are driven by strong winds, they are steered by

The Gift of Values

a very small rudder wherever the pilot wants to go. Likewise the tongue is a small part of the body, but it makes great boasts. Consider what a great forest is set on fire by such a small spark! The tongue also is a fire, a world of evil among the parts of the body. It corrupts the whole person, sets the whole course of his life on fire, and is itself set on fire by hell." *James 3:3-6 NIV*

- "But no man can tame the tongue. It is a restless evil, full of deadly poison." *James 3:7 NIV*

- "Do not use harmful words, but only helpful words, the kind that build up and provide what is needed, so that what you say will do good to those who hear you." *Ephesians 4:29 TEV*

Dig Deeper

- Watch the Veggie Tales DVD *The Ballad of Little Joe*. It has a bonus movie called *Larryboy and the Fib from Outer Space*. A little fib turns into a big problem with Junior Asparagus.

- Enjoy *Anne of Green Gables* DVD or book with your children. One of Anne's greatest challenges is learning to think before she speaks. The other is learning to control her temper. Watch for the episode where she loses her temper and breaks her slate over Gilbert Blythe's head. The books are full of examples where Anne wrestles with her quick tongue and quick temper and has to pay the price.

The Boy with Gifted Hands

"Carson, that was one of the most stupid things you've said all year!" taunted Jerry as Ben tried to escape down the school corridor. Ben shrugged, but muttered under his breath, "You've said some pretty dumb things yourself."

"What did you just say?" snarled Jerry as he drew himself to his full height. He was a good deal taller and heavier than Ben.

Ben tried to calm things down by ignoring him. He turned his back and began to work the combination lock on his locker. Just as he lifted the lock, Jerry gave him a strong shove. Ben stumbled and fell against the locker. A white hot anger surged through him. Without thinking, he swung his arm and hit Jerry with the lock as hard as he could. Jerry groaned and staggered backwards, as blood began to seep from a three inch gash on his forehead. He put his hand to his head, and then looked at the blood that covered his hand. He began to scream.

"What on earth were you doing, Carson?" demanded the principal, when Ben sat before him in his office.

"I'm so sorry, Sir," replied Ben, and he meant it. "It was *almost* an accident. I would never have hit him if I'd remembered I was holding the lock in my hand." Shame washed over him as he saw the reproach in the principal's eyes. Shame for the terrible temper that at times surged through him and made him do things he bitterly regretted later. Ben looked down at the floor and closed his eyes. And as the principal drummed his fingers lightly on the desk, different unwanted memories flooded Ben's mind. Like the time a young boy had thrown a stone at him on the way home from school. It hadn't hurt at all, but nevertheless he had felt an irrational rage and had picked up a rock and hurled it at the boy. Ben shrugged his shoulders as if trying to rid himself of the memory of the boy's broken glasses and bleeding nose. But worse than that - in a fit of rage he had nearly struck his mother. And all over some stupid trousers she had bought him that he was too embarrassed to wear. If his brother hadn't caught his arm in time, he would have hit his own mother. Ben felt like groaning.

"Look at me, Ben," said the principal.

Ben dragged his eyes from the floor and made himself look the principal in the eye.

"You're fourteen years old, with all your life ahead of you. It's up to you what you make of it. But one thing's for sure. You are going to have to get control of your anger, or it will destroy you."

Ben left the principal's office determined to make a change for the better. But somehow, it wasn't that easy.

A year later, Ben sat with his friend listening to the radio.

"Call that music?" laughed Bob, as he reached out and turned the dial to another station.

Irritated, Ben grabbed the dial and turned it back to his station. "It's better than the stuff you like!" he growled.

"Come on, Carson. You always…"

At that moment something snapped inside Ben. A blind rage took hold of him. Grabbing his camping knife out of his back pocket, he snapped it open and lunged at his friend. He thrust the knife at his belly with all his strength. The knife hit Bob's big, heavy buckle with such force that the blade snapped and fell on the ground. It all happened in a couple of seconds.

Shocked, Ben froze where he was and stared at the broken blade on the ground. The enormity of what had just happened began to sink into his mind. *I almost killed him. I almost killed my best friend.*

Bob stared at his friend in disbelief without saying a word.

"I'm… sorry," whispered Ben. Then he turned and fled.

When he reached the house, he ran into the bathroom and slammed the door. Sinking onto the floor, he put his head on his knees and tried to stop shaking. *I nearly killed Bob. I must be crazy.*

Over and over, he heard the sickening sound of the blade snapping, and saw the look of horror on his friend's face. His stomach churned inside and he felt like he was going to throw up. He hated himself. *How could it have come to this? Since I was eight years old I've dreamed of being a doctor. And here I am - I've just tried to stab my best friend. Oh God, please, You've got to help me. I can't do this on my own. Please, Lord. Take this temper from me. If you don't, I'll never be free from it.*

Tears streamed down his face. How could he ever change? He'd heard people say you can never change the type of person you are. But Ben also knew about God. His mother had taught him to pray. Well, if ever he needed God, it was now. *Please, God. You can change me. You can set me free.*

For two hours Ben sat on the bathroom floor, shaking and crying and praying. Then a verse from Proverbs came into his mind: "He who is slow to anger is better than the mighty, and he who rules his own spirit than he who takes a city." The words condemned him, but they also gave him hope.

A deep peace began to wash over him. His shaking stopped and a feeling of lightness flooded his body. He felt different. Washed inside. Free. Ben stood up and went to the sink and splashed his face with cold water. He looked at himself in the mirror and said out loud, "My temper will never control me again. Never again. I'm free."

When Ben Carson walked out of the bathroom, he was a changed young man. Never again did he have a problem with his temper. He went on to excel at medical school, and then became one the most celebrated neurosurgeons in the world. The young boy who nearly took the life of his best friend, went on to save countless lives in the operating room and to work miracles on children others had written off as hopeless.

Think About It

- What was Ben Carson's problem?
- What happened each time he became angry?
- Why did the principal tell Ben his anger would destroy him?
- What stopped him from killing his friend?
- How did he finally get free from his terrible temper?
- God had a wonderful plan for Ben Carson's life. What was it?

Something To Do

- Read the account of Cain and Abel in *Genesis 4:3-12*. Point out to the children that God warned Cain. "Why are you so angry? Why is your face downcast? If you do what is right, will you not be accepted? But if you do not do what is right, sin is crouching at your door; it desires to have you, but you must master it." That last phrase is such a powerful statement. I have used it a number of times when trying to convince a child of the absolute necessity of changing their attitude. You must master it. Get control of your anger. Your jealousy. Don't let it devour you. Cry out to the Lord for help. Ask Him to give you the strength to master it.

- Discuss the quote, 'I am indeed a king, because I know how to rule myself.' (Pietro Aretino) Then make a crown together out of cardboard and decorate it with gold paint and jewels. Present it each evening to the child who has mastered his temper and controlled his anger. Perhaps the 'king' can be entitled to certain privileges the following day?

- Think together of strategies you can use to control your temper. Some might be as simple as counting to ten (or a hundred!); moving away from whatever is making you feel angry; taking some deep breaths.

Self Control

- Discuss together the Chinese proverb that says, "If you are patient in one moment of anger, you will escape a hundred days of sorrow."

- You'll have to wait till dark for this activity. Gather your children into a darkened room and then turn off the light. Then turn on a lantern. Explain to them that Jesus wants us to be lights shining in the darkness. (*Matthew 5*) Then drape a single layer of black cloth over the lantern. The light will be dimmed. Then double the cloth over it again. Do this a few times until the light has been blocked completely. Explain to them that this is what happens if we hold anger in our hearts. Anger never remains static. If we don't deal with it, it grows. Then take the cloth off the lantern and let the light shine out again. Explain that God wants us to shine like a light in a dark place, but we can't shine for Him if we nurse anger in our hearts.

- Teach your older children how to do a scan and defragmentation on your computer's hard drive. (Or maybe ask them to teach you!) Explain to them that dealing with anger is like that - cleaning up our inner workings so that we can function properly.

- In 1867 Horatio Palmer wrote a song that was sung for many years in Sunday Schools. It would be a great one for your older children to memorise as a poem.

> *"Angry words are lightly spoken*
> *In a rash and thoughtless hour;*
> *Brightest links of life are broken*
> *By their deep, insidious power.*
>
> *Hearts inspired by warmest feeling*
> *Ne'er before by anger stirred,*
> *Oft are rent past human healing*
> *By a single angry word.*

The Gift of Values

Poison-drops of care and sorrow,
Bitter poison drops are they,
Weaving for the coming morrow
Saddest memories of today.

Angry words, oh, let them never
From the tongue unbridled slip.
May the heart's best impulse ever,
Check them ere they soil the lip.

Love is much too pure and holy,
Friendship is too sacred far,
For a moment's reckless folly
Thus to desolate and mar.

Angry words are lightly spoken,
Bitterest thoughts are rashly stirred,
Brightest links of life are broken
By a single angry word."

Horatio R. Palmer

So Said...

- "Save your breath to cool your porridge." *Anon*
- "Anger is a stone thrown into a wasp's nest." *Anon*
- "My fault, my failure, is not in the passions I have, but in my lack of control of them." *Jack Kerouac*
- "When passion drives you, let reason hold the reins." *Benjamin Franklin*
- "The greatest enemy for anger is delay." *Seneca*
- "He who angers you, conquers you." *Elizabeth Kenny*

- ❖ "We mustn't let our passions destroy our dreams." *Anon*
- ❖ "He who reigns within himself, and rules passions, desires, fears, is more than a king." *John Milton*
- ❖ "Anyone can be angry. That is easy. But to be angry with the right person, to the right degree, at the right time, for the right reason and in the right way - that is not easy." *Aristotle*

Boom Clip

Over the years, we have had to constantly remind one of our more fiesty children to control their temper. The other children have heard the phrase, 'control your temper' many times. The other day Sam and Jake were playing together in the lounge, and Sam must have got a bit annoyed at his younger brother. The next minute we heard Jacob's little voice saying, "Sam! Obey your temper!"

Words To Live By

- ❖ A fool gives full vent to his anger, but a wise man keeps himself under control." *Proverbs 29:11 NIV*
- ❖ "A patient man has great understanding, but a quick-tempered man displays folly." *Proverbs 14:29 NIV*
- ❖ "A wise man fears the Lord and shuns evil, but a fool is hot-headed and reckless. A quick-tempered man does foolish things." *Proverbs 14:16,17 NIV*
- ❖ "A hot-tempered man stirs up dissension, but a patient man calms a quarrel." *Proverbs 15:18 NIV*

The Gift of Values

- "Do not make friends with a hot-tempered man, do not associate with one easily angered, or you may learn his ways and get yourself ensnared." *Proverbs 22:24,25 NIV*

- "My dear brothers, take note of this: Everyone should be quick to listen, slow to speak and slow to become angry, for man's anger does not bring about the righteous life that God desires." *James 1:19,20 NIV*

Boom Clip

In 1870 my great-great grandfather, Richard Fitzsimons, died of tuberculosis at the age of 46. Shortly before his death he wrote the following letter to his only son, John, urging him to live whole-heartedly for Christ. One of the things he mentions is how to control anger.

"To my only son I leave little indeed of earthly possessions, but an honest name of which he has no cause to be ashamed. He is well aware that from his earliest infancy I devoted him to the Lord my God, to serve Him in the Gospel of His son. This is still my earnest hope, nor need he be discouraged at the thought that little earthly comfort may attend him therein, for God is amply able to repay outward trouble with inward peace and joy in the Holy Ghost. I say to him therefore, to avoid through life all bad company, but seek to honour and follow the word of God.

Never do evil in the hope of it remaining concealed, for there is nothing so cunningly hid but it will come to light.

Do not be angry beyond what duty and office require. If you feel that you are heated with passion, keep wholly silent. Do not utter one word until you have repeated over in your own mind the Ten Commandments and the creed.

Do good to others whether they can recompense you or not; for what men cannot repay, the Maker of the world has long ago repaid in creating you, sending His Son to redeem you and receiving you by baptism into His church upon earth.

Flee covetousness as you would hell. Content yourself with what you can earn with honour and a good conscience although it may not amount to much. And should the Almighty bestow more upon you, pray to Him to preserve you from making bad use of earthly treasure.

Be instant in prayer, follow after things that are honest and of good report, save faithfully, remain steadfast in your confession, and then when your time comes you will die willingly, and joyfully."

What sage advice! So simple, and yet so powerful.

Dig Deeper

❖ A wonderful read-aloud book is *On to Oregon!* by Honore Morrow. John Sager, at age thirteen, is ready for just about any danger on his way to Oregon with his family. However he resents being given orders, but soon realises that angry feelings get him nowhere.

❖ Read *I Was So Mad* by Mercer Mayer with your younger children. Mom won't let Little Critter keep frogs in the bathtub or practice his juggling with eggs, so he decides he's going to run away.

❖ Get your older children to search the internet for the story about Alexander the Great and his friend, Cleitus. Alexander kills his best friend in a drunken brawl. Although he mourned his friend excessively and nearly committed suicide when he realised what he had done, all of Alexander's associates thereafter feared his paranoia and dangerous temper. From that time on, his men lost respect for him.

❖ A great book for parents to read is *Insight into Anger* by Wendy Bray and Chris Ledger. It's easy to read and well set out, and has a very clear message.

The Gift of Values

- ❖ Watch the DVD *Bobby Jones: A Stroke of Genius* with your older children. Bobby Jones very quickly earned the nickname 'club thrower'. An old gentleman, Grandpa Bart, recognized his potential as well as his character issues, and told Jones, "Bobby, you're good enough to win, but you'll never win big until you control that temper of yours." The film shows Bobby's rise to greatness, as well as the struggles he had to control with his fiery temper. Grandpa Bart later said, "Bobby was 14 when he mastered golf, but he was 21 when he mastered himself."

- ❖ A great read-aloud story is *The Bronze Bow* by Elizabeth Speare. Daniel is a Jewish boy whose one consuming passion is his hatred for the Romans for killing his parents. Eventually he comes to see that his real enemy is not the Romans but the hatred festering in his own heart.

- ❖ Encourage your older children to read *Gifted Hands* by Ben Carson. It tells the inspiring story of the ghetto kid from Detroit who became one of the most respected neurosurgeons in the world. He is a wonderful role model for teenagers, and his life shows us all that we can change.

Value Four

COMPASSION

Compassion. It's such a beautiful word. It brings to mind pictures of a loving mother kissing a scraped knee and cuddling a crying child; of the gentle, tender look on the face of someone watching a loved one in pain; of Christ weeping at the graveside of his friend Lazarus. The Concise Oxford Dictionary describes compassion as 'suffering with another; pity; sympathy for the sufferings and sorrows of others; an act of pity or mercy.' Compassion takes its stand with others in their distress.

Some years ago, Chris and I stayed at a friend's bach for the weekend. A storm blew in from the sea, and I settled down in a cosy armchair to read a Reader's Digest. I became engrossed in the inspiring story of a lady in England who was deeply moved one morning by a news bulletin that featured the killing fields of Cambodia. She watched in horror as they showed evidence of Pol Pot's regime of terror.

All that day as she went about her housework, she thought about what she'd seen, and prayed for the gentle people of Cambodia. That evening, when her husband came home, she shared the story with him. And then she asked him a life-changing question. "Isn't there something we can do?"

Her husband was a Methodist minister, so he suggested, "Let's organise a prayer meeting."

That week, a dozen people met in their lounge to pray for Cambodia. As they poured out their hearts in prayer, the Lord spoke to the couple's own son. *I want you to go to Cambodia.*

The Gift of Values

And so he did! He left his job and family and went to the war-ravaged country. And eleven people back home in England prayed for him daily and supported him financially. This young man was later awarded the OBE for his work of compassion among the war victims of Cambodia.

All this happened, because his mother was moved with compassion. But she had done more than cry a few tears. She had *asked* if there was something she could do. In doing so, she set into motion a wonderful chain of events.

Several years ago I went with Kate to Texas to do some concerts. We sang at Mercy Ships International, and I was thrilled to meet so many people who were giving their skills and time to reach out to some of the neediest nations of the world. We had the privilege of spending some time with Don Stephens, the founder of Mercy Ships, and he shared with us how God had worked compassion into his heart through all the trials and heartaches he and his wife had been through with their intellectually disabled son.

He also shared the story of a severely disfigured man who was found by one of the ship's medical teams. When one of the team members reached out to touch him, he shrank away and then began to cry. When he could finally speak, he told them that no human being had touched him for ten years. How terribly sad. It reminded me that, while it is easy for us to feel overwhelmed by the oceans of need we see in the world, we must never forget that Jesus reached out to people one by one.

In this chapter you will meet people whose lives were moved with compassion. People who not only saw the needs around them, but who allowed compassion to motivate them into action. May your heart be moved with compassion also.

CS

Ninepence

ladys Aylward pushed the wayward strand of hair out of her eyes and stopped to catch her breath. The mountain rose steeply before her. But as she gazed back down the narrow mountain path, she felt a great sense of adventure and fulfillment. She loved the treks she made into the mountains of China. This is what she'd spent years dreaming about back in England, as she saved every penny she could for her one-way fare to China.

With a smile on her face, she picked up her small bag and began to climb again.

She didn't notice the Chinese woman sitting by the side of the track until she was almost upon her.

"Oh, hello," said Gladys, smiling warmly at the young woman. The lady stared coldly back at her, and then glanced down at her lap. Gladys followed her eyes down to a small bundle of dirty rags lying across the woman's crossed legs. The woman pulled at part of the cloth, and Gladys heard a tiny whimper. A prickle of understanding shot through her body. The bundle of rags contained a small child. She stifled a gasp. The woman smiled at her in a slow, aggravating way.

"Do you want to buy the child?" she asked. "I don't want it."

Gladys swallowed hard. The woman watched her, aware of the effect her words had on the white woman's feelings. "It will die if you don't take it. How much will you pay me?"

"Whose child is it?" asked Gladys. She knew all too well that children and even babies were sometimes kidnapped by heartless people who used them to make their begging more effective.

The woman shrugged her shoulders. "How much?" she asked again.

"I only have ninepence," said Gladys angrily.

"Ninepence will have to do," replied the woman, holding out her hand.

Gladys reached into her bag and pulled out the money.

The Gift of Values

Her hands shook as she gathered up the bundle of rags and held the child to her chest. "Hello, little Ninepence," she whispered. "You are safe with me."

One year later, Ninepence walked into the house at dinnertime, leading a small boy by the hand. "Can he stay, please?" she asked Gladys. "I will eat less so that he can have something."

And so it was that another needy child found his way into the heart and home of Gladys Aylward - a little abandoned boy who they named 'Less.'

Think About It

- ❖ Why did the woman want to sell the child?
- ❖ How much did Gladys pay for the child?
- ❖ Was that all this act of compassion cost Gladys? (No. From that time on, she had to care for Ninepence, feed her, clothe her, and mother her. Compassion will always cost.)
- ❖ How did Gladys' compassion affect Ninepence? (Ninepence also reached out in love to the needy. Compassion always has a ripple effect.)
- ❖ Why did they call the little boy, 'Less'?

Something To Do

- Choose to sponsor a child as a family through Tear Fund or World Vision. The children can write to their child, send small gifts and pray for them.

- Get your older children to search the internet and find the story of how World Vision began. Bob Pierce came across a young child, just as Gladys Aylward did.

- Discuss together the problem of beggars. So much need. So many beggars - some of them professional, but many of them in real need and poverty. The scale of it can be numbing and can make people harden their hearts and refuse to part with a cent. If you've been overseas and experienced what it's like to have a dirty child thrust their hand into your taxi and beg for some money, share it with your children. Tell them how you felt. Ask your children what they would do. Would they give them some money? All of it? What about their own hotel bill? How do you cope with walking down a street and being accosted by beggars at every corner?

  After my first experience in Nepal I decided I would never go there unprepared again. I determined that I would prayerfully set aside a certain amount of money, which would be exclusively for giving to beggars. And that, each morning before I went out on the streets, I would ask the Lord to show me to whom I should give. With each gift, I would tell the person about the Lord as much as I was able. It was amazing the difference it made. I no longer felt overwhelmed by the need - rather, it became an exciting adventure each day.

- Read together *Deuteronomy 15:7-11* To be compassionate is to have a soft heart, an open hand. We must not harden our hearts when we see need. Rather, we must ask God to soften our hearts.

The Gift of Values

- Read the parable of the Good Samaritan in *Luke 10:29 - 37*. This is a great one to act out!

- Do a research project on Florence Nightingale.

- Memorize together the prayer of St Francis of Assisi.

Lord, make me an instrument of Thy peace;
Where there is hatred, let me sow love;
Where there is injury, pardon; where there is doubt, faith;
Where there is despair, hope: where there is darkness, light;
Where there is sadness, joy.
Oh Divine Master,
Grant that I may not so much seek to be consoled as to console;
To be understood as to understand: to be loved, as to love.
For it is giving that we receive;
It is in pardoning that we are pardoned,
And it is in dying that we are born to eternal life.

So Said...

- "I am only one; but still I am one. I cannot do everything, but still I can do something. I will not refuse to do the something I can do." *Helen Keller*

- "Never lose sight of the 'ones.' One sheep, one coin, one son." *Anon*

- "One by one we are born; one by one we feel pain; one by one are healed by love." *Sandy (Mercy Ships)*

- "I became permanently impressed with the kindness of the poor to each other: the woman who lives upstairs will willingly share her breakfast with the family below because she knows they are 'hard up'; the man who boarded with them last winter will give a month's rent because he knows the father of the family is out of work; the baker across the street who is fast being pushed to the wall by his downtown competitors, will send across three loaves of stale bread because he has seen the children looking longingly into his window and suspects they are hungry…" *Jane Addams*

- "We cannot tell the precise moment when friendship is formed. As in filling a vessel drop by drop, there is at last a drop, which makes it run over. So in a series of acts of kindness, there is, at last, one which makes the heart run over." *James Boswell*

- "I am trying to help street children because I understand their life. I was everything they are. All I needed was a chance. All I needed was for someone to love me, to believe in me, and to give me a chance. All I needed was one friend, one person who did not reject me." *Christina Noble* (*Bridge Across my Sorrows*)

- "When I first came to Vietnam, people said what I wanted to do was impossible. 'You are only one person,' they said. But when I was a child, I needed only one person to understand my suffering and pain, one person to love me. One is very important. There are many ones, and they add up. Sometimes people sit in their homes and they are bored and they say, 'I don't know what to do.' I say to them, 'Go outside your home. Visit the orphanages; go and talk to people on the street, and every time you see someone who is poor or homeless,' ask yourself, 'If that was my brother or my father or my child, what would I do?'" *Christina Noble* (*Bridge Across my Sorrows*)

The Gift of Values

- "I came upon a doctor who appeared in quite poor health. I said, 'There's nothing that I can do that you can't do for yourself.' He said, 'Oh yes, you can. Just hold my hand. I think that would help.' So I sat with him for a while then I asked him how he felt. He said, 'I think I'm cured.'" *Conor Oberst*

- "Compassion will cure more sins than condemnation." *Henry Ward Beecher*

- "Man may dismiss compassion from his heart, but God never will." *William Cowper*

Boom Clip

I sat outside in the spring sunshine, revelling in its warmth. It was a beautiful morning. All of a sudden unbidden, my mind filled with images I had recently seen on television news. And at the same time, my heart was swamped with the same emotion I had felt when I had first seen them. I began to weep. I jumped up and ran inside, found a scrap of paper and began to write. The words poured out of me.

Saw the heart-rending sight of the Kurds on their flight
And a father who wept for his son
Saw the grief on his face
Felt a pain that was laced
With despair over what could be done
Saw the pitiful sight of a young baby's fight
With cancer, Chernobyl's claim
And the helpless tears, the young mother's fears
Stirred an anger in me for their pain

Compassionate heart that moves me to pray
Moves me to ask Lord what is my part?
What can I do? Where can I go?
Let my tears be just the start
Father, teach me to pray; compel me to give
Let compassion forge a new reason to live
Let love determine my day

Saw the sad photograph of the precious wee feet
Of a ten-week-old unborn child
So perfect and tiny yet sacrificed hourly
To a selfish world that's gone wild

I saw the hot dry tears of a mother who held
A starving child to her breast
Saw the big wide eyes and the pitiful size
Felt a pain trapped deep in my chest
We feel so helpless, we feel so useless
We feel so powerless but we are not!
Our prayers, our money, our lives, our talents
We each have something that they haven't got

Compassionate heart that moves me to pray
Moves me to ask, Lord, what is my part?
What can I do? Where can I go?
Let my tears be just the start
Father, teach me to pray; compel me to give
Let compassion forge a new reason to live
Let love determine my day.

(You can listen to this song on our web site *www.boomfamily.co.nz*)

The Gift of Values

When our hearts are deeply moved as we feel someone else's pain, we are experiencing the God-given gift of compassion. But it's not enough for us to simply cry a few tears and then wipe them away. God gives us compassion as a motivator; compassion urges us to *do* something to help; it moves us into action. When we experience the emotion of compassion, we need to follow through by taking action. When Jesus saw the crowds like sheep without a shepherd, He felt compassion for them - and He fed them, He healed them, and He preached the good news of God's forgiveness and love to them.

Words To Live By

❖ "Have mercy on me, O God, according to your unfailing love; according to your great compassion blot out my transgressions." *Psalm 51:1 NIV*

❖ "But you are a forgiving God, gracious and compassionate, slow to anger and abounding in love... Because of your great compassion you did not abandon them in the desert." *Nehemiah 9:17, 19 NIV* (Read on through to *verse 21* to see the outworking of God's great compassion.)

❖ "Praise the Lord, O my soul, and forget not all his benefits - who forgives all your sins and heals all your diseases, who redeems your life from the pit and crowns you with love and compassion, who satisfies your desires with good things so that your youth is renewed like the eagle's." *Psalm 103:2 -5 NIV*

❖ "The Lord is gracious and righteous; our God is full of compassion." *Psalm 116:5 NIV*

❖ "Yet the Lord longs to be gracious to you; He rises to show you compassion." *Isaiah 30:18 NIV*

❖ "Because of the Lord's great love we are not consumed, for his compassions never fail. They are new every morning; great is your faithfulness." *Lamentations 3:22,23 NIV*

❖ "But while he was still a long way off, his father saw him and was filled with compassion for him; he ran to his son, threw his arms around him and kissed him." *Luke 15:20 NIV*

❖ "A righteous man cares for the needs of his animal." *Proverbs 12:10 NIV* (The need for compassion also extends to animals.)

Boom Clip

Chris and I were in India for World Vision. Our hearts were deeply touched by the different people we met who had worked hard to get a degree, and then come returned to the slums to work with World Vision among the poor. One of these was a young man named Joseph. He was a slight man, with a beautiful open face and a very white smile. As we drove around Calcutta, he told us his story. He was born into a very poor Hindu family. But when he was aged seven, he was chosen as a sponsored child with World Vision. His sponsor wrote to him from Canada saying, "Joseph, I'm so glad I can be a part of your life. I live in Canada and am training to be a doctor. Now you might think I'm very rich, but I'm not. I'm going without lunch each day so I can pay for you to get an education. Make the most of this opportunity, Joseph! Do your very best at school. And I will be praying every day that the Lord will touch your heart and use you for His glory."

Joseph treasured that letter and hung it on the wall of the small shack that was his home. While he was still very young he became a Christian, and from that time on, he knew that one day he would come back to his own slums and give to them the young Canadian doctor had given to him. He worked hard at school and eventually graduated with a degree in business. He was offered a high paying job in Madras but it didn't tempt him one little bit.

"I am living proof that the work of World Vision changes lives!" he told us with a big grin.

What an inspiration! One young man was moved with compassion and did something… and the ripples go on and on.

Dig Deeper

- Read together *Flight of the Fugitives* by Dave and Neta Jackson. It tells the story of Gladys Aylward, missionary to China, and her daring attempt to rescue a hundred orphans from the approaching Japanese army.

- Watch the DVD *Molokai* with your older children. It's the inspiring story of a monk who chooses to go and live among the lepers in order to share the gospel with them.

- Watch the DVD *Mother Teresa* with your older children.

- Visit *www.joniandfriends.org/pressbox/Lausanne.pdf* and read a wonderful article about compassion written by Joni Eareckson Tada. A thought provoking read for your teenagers.

- Read with your younger children *The Good Samaritan* in the *Ready to Read Series* by Nick and Claire Page.

- Read *The Lion and the Mouse* from Aesop's Fables with your younger children. It illustrates the powerful truth that compassion lies within the power of both the mighty and the weak, and that the ripples of compassion return to bless the compassionate.

- Read *Androcles and the Lion*, a slightly more complicated version of the fable of The Lion and the Mouse. A beautiful truth illustrated in this fable is that Androcles, a slave, is able to feel compassion for another's suffering despite having been so cruelly mistreated himself.

- Read *Little Thumbelina* by Hans Christian Andersen. It teaches little children how to have big hearts.

- Watch the DVD *Beauty and the Beast*. It is a beautiful example of love growing from compassion.

- ❖ Encourage your older children to read *Ten Fingers for God* by Dorothy Clarke Wilson. It tells about the life and work of Dr Paul Brand, the man whose surgical techniques brought blessing and hope to countless thousands of leprosy patients. His parents were missionaries in India, and he learned at an early age what it was to feel compassion for the poor and forsaken.

- ❖ Read *The Dangerous Voyage* (one of the Reel Kids Adventure series) by Dave Gustaveson. Jeff and the Reel Kids are off on a mercy ship to help hurricane victims in Haiti.

- ❖ Read *The Drummer Boy's Battle* by Dave and Neta Jackson. Twelve-year-old Robbie is a drummer boy in the Crimean war. When he is injured, he meets the lady with the lamp - Florence Nightingale, the nurse ighting to change the conditions in hospitals.

- ❖ Read *Mystery at Smokey Mountain* by Dave Gustaveson. Compassion motivates Jeff and the Reel Kids to go to help the poor at Smokey Mountain in Manila.

The Gift of Values

William and the Ring

illiam looked up from his work when the doorbell rang. A pale woman entered the shop, with a young lad trailing beside her. William guessed the boy would be about thirteen, his own age. He smiled at him, but the lad kept his eyes on the floor, and his back slightly turned to him. William felt a deep sadness. Time and time again he'd seen the same look of shame and embarrassment on the faces of those who entered the pawnshop. He hated his job. Ever since his father had been thrown into the pauper's prison, William had been working in the pawnshop. And every time a poor person came through its door, the bell jangled in William's very soul.

The woman cleared her throat, and William jumped at the sound.

"I'm sorry," he stammered. "Forgive me. How can I help you?"

The lady brushed away a dark strand of hair from her eyes, and then laid a small leather pouch on the bench top. William watched her thin fingers shake as she struggled to undo the knot. At length she freed the drawstring and tipped the contents on the counter. A single ring fell out. William hesitated. He didn't even want to touch it. His own hands trembled as he picked it up and held it to the light. It was made of pure gold. A small solitary ruby glowed in the centre. William turned the ring over in his hands. *It's way too big for her bony finger,* thought William, *but it probably used to fit.* He remembered watching his own mother's soft face become sunken and sharp.

"How much can you give me for it?" asked the woman. William glanced up at her. She was watching him with dull, sad eyes. The boy had turned his back completely and stood nervously twisting the side of his baggy shirt.

"Well, Ma'am," began William, and he cleared his own throat nervously. "I'm afraid we're not in the position to offer you nearly as much as this ring is worth." He reached into the drawer and pulled out a few small coins. He counted them out and laid them on the bench top. His hands felt sweaty.

He wiped them on his shirt as the woman slowly counted the money. Once, twice.

"Is this all?" she asked in a small voice.

William's eyes flicked to the tightly hunched shoulders of the young boy. "I'm afraid so, Ma'am. I wish I could give you more. But I'm afraid I…" His voice trailed off as he glanced to the back of the shop. God knows, if he had a pocketful of gold, he would have poured it all into her hands at that moment. But he didn't.

"I see. Thank you," said the woman. William heard the edge of pride in her quiet voice. "I'll take the money."

He watched silently as she dropped the coins into the leather pouch, and drew the drawstring tight. Then she gave him a tremulous smile, and turned to leave the shop. She gathered her son towards her with an arm around his shoulders, and together they walked out of the shop and out of William's life.

William let out a soft groan. He knew by now that very few who pawned their treasures were ever able to buy them back.

"One day," whispered William to the window display of watches and necklaces and rings. "One day, I'll do something to help change all this."

And he did. After his conversion, young William Booth's greatest goal in life became helping the poor. During the long, hard hours he spent working in the pawnshop, he developed a deep compassion for their plight. He understood the pain and suffering caused by poverty. He knew all too well the terrible effect the gin shops had on the families of London's East End. William began preaching to anyone who would listen. He shared about God's love to the ragged urchins that ran wild in the streets, and soon had a large following of thin, dirty children. However, when he took them to church, the well-dressed, wealthy people were displeased. The deacons moved William and the boys to a place in the church where the respectable folk couldn't see them.

The Gift of Values

William began to dream of starting a church for the poor. A place where they would be welcomed and cared for. The dream grew and developed. William married Catherine, a young girl who shared the same passion for souls and the same concern for the poor. Together they formed one of the world's greatest compassionate societies - the Salvation Army.

Think About It

- Why did William have to work in the pawnshop?
- What was a paupers' prison?
- How did William Booth work to help the poor?
- Are there poor people in our cities? Our country? Who are they?
- Did William Booth only preach the gospel to the poor? (No, he also tried to meet their physical needs.)

Something To Do

- Brainstorm together for ways your family could help the poor. Consider practical things, not just giving money.
- Get involved in any local outreach your church may have for the poor. Soup kitchens, meals, gardening.
- Each try and earn some money that you will give to help the poor. Offer some rewards for jobs around the house, and make sure you have some that are suitable for your pre-schoolers. It's never too early to start encouraging your children to help other people. Make sure they understand the principle of the widow's mite - that it's not the size of the gift that counts. God sees the heart.

❖ Take your children with you on a short-term mission trip. It will be life-changing. I know it costs a lot of money - more than you think you could ever save - but it's worth every cent! I took a team of nine teenagers, including two of my own children, on a mission trip to the Yasawa Islands last year. They all worked hard for about ten months to raise their fares. We mowed lawns, baby sat, sold chocolates, busked on the streets, held a charity auction, put on an Indian dinner and countless other things. And the money came in! We had a fantastic three weeks onboard the mercy ship *Pacific Link*. It was a life-changing time for all of us.

Boom Clip

The Indian dinner and auction to raise money for our mission trip had been a huge success. We'd made $3,000! After the big clean-up, I stopped at an ATM to bank the money. I didn't want to risk losing it. Josiah and Kate were with me in the car; Chris had left earlier and taken the younger children home. It was about 11pm and I felt just a little nervous standing in the dark with all of the hard-earned money. Suddenly, out of the corner of my eye, I saw a white car speed up to the park beside our van and a man jump out. It all happened so fast. He ran behind me, grabbed my shoulders and growled, "Give me your money!"

There was no way I was going to let a thief run off with our precious money. I began to fight and kick as hard as I could. Then I heard the kids laughing and shouting something to me. It took a moment before I actually heard what they were shouting. "Mum, it's Dad!"

I stared at my attacker. It was Chris, looking very sheepish.

"I'm sorry," he grovelled. "I was sure you'd realise it was me."

I blinked and looked again. Slowly the truth of it sank in. I had forgotten that Chris had said he was going to pick up the work car before taking the children home. I'd forgotten he'd said he'd probably be behind me. Of course I should have recognized his voice! I was still shaking and clutching the envelope with the money.

The kids couldn't stop laughing. "Man, Mum, you're fierce!" giggled Jacob.

Chris looked like he wanted to laugh but didn't dare. Slowly the adrenaline drained away. I grinned at him. "Don't you ever frighten me like that again!" I warned. "And you'd better stay with me while I bank this money!"

So Said...

- ❖ "While women weep, as they do now, I'll fight; while children go hungry, as they do now I'll fight; while men go to prison, in and out, in and out, as they do now, I'll fight; while there is a drunkard left, while there is a poor lost girl upon the streets, while there remains one dark soul without the light of God, I'll fight, I'll fight to the very end!" *General William Booth*

- ❖ "I must assert in the most unqualified way that it is primarily and mainly for the sake of saving the soul that I seek the salvation of the body." *General William Booth*

- ❖ "Brethren, do something, do something, do something!" *Charles Spurgeon*

- ❖ "There never was a heart truly great and generous that was not also tender and compassionate." *Robert Frost*

Boom Clip

While I was searching for verses about compassion, I heard a whimper coming towards me. I looked up and saw Milly coming into the study, clutching her arm. She had tears in her eyes as she showed me a scratch from the bookshelf. As I hugged her and kissed her, I felt such a love for my little girl. No matter that it was just a simple scratch. All Milly needed was a hug and a kiss and then she was right as rain. As she ran off to play, I realised the Lord feels compassion at our slightest hurt and sadness, not just at our deepest pain. Why? Because He loves us! It amazes me how whenever one of our little ones is hurt, their first thought is to go to Mummy or Daddy. It's like they're drawn to us by some invisible cord. And every time they come, it is our opportunity to show them the compassion of God.

Words To Live By

- ❖ "I tell you, open your eyes and look at the fields! They are ripe for harvest." *John 4:35 NIV*

- ❖ "Everyone who calls on the name of the Lord will be saved. How, then, can they call on the one they have not believed in? And how can they believe in the one of whom they have not heard? And how can they hear without someone preaching to them? And how can they preach unless they are sent? As it is written, 'How beautiful on the mountains are the feet of those who bring good news!'" *Romans 10:13-15 NIV*

- ❖ "Go out quickly into the streets and alleys of the town and bring in the poor, the crippled, the blind and the lame." *Luke 14:21 NIV* (NB We are to search out the disabled and share with them God's love!)

- ❖ "Jesus went through all the towns and villages, teaching in their synagogues, preaching the good news of the kingdom and healing every disease and sickness. When he saw the crowds, He had compassion on them, because they were harassed and helpless, like sheep without a shepherd." *Matthew 9:35,36 NIV*

- ❖ "When Jesus landed and saw a large crowd, he had compassion on them and healed their sick." *Matthew 14:14 NIV*

The Gift of Values

- "Great crowds came to Him, bringing the lame, the blind, the crippled, the mute and many others, and laid them at His feet: and He healed them. The people were amazed when they saw the mute speaking; the crippled made well, the lame walking and the blind seeing. And they praised the God of Israel. Jesus called His disciples to Him and said, 'I have compassion for these people; they have already been with me three days and have nothing to eat. I do not want to send them away hungry, or they may collapse on the way." *Matthew 15:30-33 NIV* (Ask the children if they know what miracle Jesus did then. He fed the four thousand.)

Dig Deeper

- Read *The Hidden Jewel* by Dave and Neta Jackson. It's the story of a young boy who moves to India and befriends the Irish missionary, Amy Carmichael. Soon he is embroiled in all sorts of adventures as he helps her rescue a young Indian girl from the temple.

- Read *Trial by Poison* by Dave and Neta Jackson. It's the exciting story of Mary Slessor, who was inspired by the story of David Livingstone to leave Scotland and become a missionary to Africa. She fought against the murder of twins, slavery and human sacrifice.

- Read the inspiring story of Harriet Tubman in *Listen for the Whippoorwill* by Dave and Neta Jackson. Compassion for the plight of the slaves compelled her to risk her own life many times to help them escape to freedom.

- Read *Florence Nightingale* by David and Patricia Armentrout from the *People who Made a Difference* series. At seventeen she wrote in her diary that she felt called by God to a life of service.

- Read *The Princess and Curdie* by George MacDonald. A lovely story of a young miner boy who is called upon to save the king and the princess.

- Read *Black Beauty* by Anna Sewell or watch the DVD. It deals with the issue of cruelty to animals. There are stark contrasts between the people who show compassion to Black Beauty and those who treat her with no compassion at all. A caution however - several of my tender-hearted children found the movie very upsetting in parts.

- Read *Jip: His story* by Katherine Paterson. It's the heart-warming story of a young boy who 'tumbled off the back of a wagon and was not looked for by anyone.' His compassion and love for people and animals brings hope and help to the troubled people around him.

- Read *Brady* by Jean Fritz. Young Brady Minton hasn't really given the issue of slavery any serious thought until he sees runaway slaves being hidden near his home.

- Enjoy a picture book with your younger children called *Battle at the Gate* by New Zealand author Jenny Jenkins. Heni Te Kirikaramu, a young Maori woman, is present when British troops attack Gate Pa, Tauranga in 1864. There are many casualties. Heni is moved with compassion when she hears a wounded soldier crying out for water in the night, and she tends to the hurt and dying enemy soldiers.

- Read *The Thieves of Tyburn Square* by Dave and Neta Jackson. Two young pick pockets are imprisoned for stealing, but find hope when they are visited by Elizabeth Fry, a compassionate prison reformer.

- Research the work of the Salvation Army. Your older children could read one of the many books about William and Catherine Booth. (One of my favourites is *Catherine Booth* by Catherine Bramwell Booth. An inspiring book for mothers and wives to read!)

The Gift of Values

The Watchmakers of Haarlem

he Beje's side entrance doorbell rang. A young Jewish woman stood in the alley, cradling a tiny baby in her arms. Her face looked pale and gaunt in the twilight. Behind her stood a young intern from the hospital.

"Come in, come in," urged Corrie quietly.

"The baby is premature, Corrie," explained the young doctor as they stepped into the hallway. "I kept them in the hospital for as long as I dared, seeing as they have nowhere to go. Can you help them?"

"Of course," reassured Corrie, as her sister, Betsie, held out her arms and gently took the baby.

Together they led the woman into the dining room. Corrie ladled out a bowl of soup and handed it her.

"Thank you," she whispered, as she looked up at Corrie with large brown eyes, brimming with fear.

At that moment the baby began to wail; a high thin cry that seemed to fill the room. "Shh. Shh," crooned Betsie as she rocked her gently.

That night the two sisters lay in bed and discussed the problem. A tiny child could never know the danger that lay all around. Her pathetic cries would put all the other Jews in the Beje at risk.

"We must find somewhere in the country for them," said Betsie. "Somewhere that they'll be safe."

"Ja," said Corrie. "But where? Who can we ask?"

"We must pray, Corrie," replied Betsie. "We must ask God to provide."

The next morning, Corrie felt her heart leap for joy when she saw the pastor from a small town out of Haarlem walk in the shop door. Here, for sure, was God's answer to their prayer!

She drew him out the back door of the shop and up the stairs into the dining room.

"Pastor, how glad I am that you have come! You are an answer to our prayer."

The pastor's face wrinkled into a slight frown.

Corrie continued, her words coming out in a big rush. "You have the perfect place! Would you take a young Jewish mother and her small baby into your home? They will almost certainly be arrested otherwise."

The pastor took a step backwards as if she had slapped him in the face. The colour drained from his face.

"Miss ten Boom!" he whispered, his voice tight with fear. "I hope you're not involved in any illegal, underground work! Think of your dear father, and your sister who is so unwell!"

But Corrie was not perturbed. "Please, wait here!" she cried, and she flew up the stairs to where the mother and child were hiding. Gathering the tiny bundle in her arms, she retraced her steps and walked up to the pastor. "Look!" she said tenderly, as she uncovered the blankets from the baby's face. The small face grew pink as she sucked furiously on tiny, red fists.

The pastor stared down at the infant in silence. Then he slowly reached out a hand to touch the soft cheek. Corrie watched as fear and compassion struggled in his face. Then his back stiffened and he straightened up. "No. Definitely not. We could all lose our lives for this one Jewish baby."

Corrie stared at him in disbelief. Had she heard him wrong? Instinctively she held the child tighter to her chest.

"Corrie."

She spun around to see her father standing at the door.

He limped towards her and held out his arms. "Give the child to me."

Corrie watched as her eighty-two-year-old father cradled the baby, his long white beard brushing against its soft cheek. He gazed down at the child for a long time. No one spoke. Then he looked up and fixed his clear blues eyes on the pastor.

"You say we could lose our lives for this child. I would consider that to be the greatest honour that could come to my family. The child will stay with us."

The Gift of Values

The pastor turned on his heels sharply and strode out of the room.

Corrie looked at her father with a heart bursting with happiness. Tears filled her eyes. How she loved him! He had always been the one to teach her about God and show her how to live for Him. She had watched him all her life as he reached out in compassion to the hurting, the hungry, and the lonely. She had seen him join the long queues of Jews waiting to be given the yellow star by the Germans, and watched him wear it with love for God's people. She had listened to him pour out his heart in prayer for them. But never had she loved him as much as now.

She put an arm around his shoulders and gave him a kiss on his cheek. "Ja! Papa! It is an honour indeed."

Casper ten Boom was arrested on February 28, 1944, along with his daughters, Corrie and Betsie. When he stood before the chief interrogator's desk, the Gestapo chief told him, "I'd like to send you home, old man. I'll take your word that you won't cause any more trouble."

Corrie couldn't see her father's face, but she heard his clear answer. "If I go home today, tomorrow I will open my door again to any man in need who knocks."

With an angry gesture, the chief signaled for him to be led him away, and Corrie and Betsie heard his last words to them. "God go with you, my daughters."

He died in a prison hospital corridor ten days later.

Think About It

- When would this story have been set?
- Ask the children to find the Netherlands on a map. See if they can find Haarlem.
- Why did the Jews have to wear a yellow star?
- Why were Corrie and Betsie worried about the baby?

Compassion

- What was the illegal, underground work the ten Booms were involved in?
- What did the young pastor urge Corrie to consider, as a reason to avoid becoming involved in anything too dangerous?
- Why did the pastor decide not to help the mother and child?
- Ask your children to think about what they would have done.
- What did Father ten Boom say when he held the baby?
- Did he end up giving his life to help God's people?
- Do you think he regrets his actions now?

Something To Do

- Do a project about the Ten Boom family. When we did this, Kate had a lot of fun writing the envelope with a crooked address that pointed to the stamp. And just like in Corrie's story, she had written a secret message under the stamp. 'All the watches in the cupboard are safe.' That was the code Nollie had written to let Corrie know that all the Jews hiding in the secret cupboard were safe.

- The ten Boom family and all the occupants of the Beje (say Bay yay) had a raid drill every day. In the beginning the drill took four minutes. The tricky part was that the soldiers liked to do the raids at mealtimes and in the middle of the night. These were the two times of day that people would most likely be caught off guard. During mealtime the people hiding needed to quickly go up-stairs without dropping food or other personal items, and get to the room. Meanwhile the Ten Booms needed to reset the table, and make sure there were not too many utensils on the table, paying attention to every detail. If the raid came at night the Jews needed to gather all their things, flip the mattress they were sleeping on, so that no warmth could be felt where they had lain, then

The Gift of Values

quickly and quietly get to the secret room. By the fifth drill they had got the time down to two and one half minutes, but still not to the ideal time of seventy seconds.

Choose a small space in your house where everyone has to run to and hide in when the bell goes. Everyone has to learn how to co-operate and play their part. No-one must make a sound.

❖ Research about the Dutch Underground. Compassion motivated them to risk their lives.

So Said...

❖ "Life's most urgent question is, what are you doing for others?" *Martin Luther King, Jr*

❖ "I feel the capacity to care is the thing which gives life its deepest significance." *Pablo Casals*

❖ "The value of compassion cannot be over-emphasized. Anyone can criticize. It takes a true believer to be compassionate. No greater burden can be borne by an individual than to know no one cares or understands." *Arthur H. Stainback*

❖ "The individual is capable of both great compassion and great indifference. He has it within his means to nourish the former and outgrow the latter." *Norman Cousins*

❖ "If I can stop one heart from breaking, I shall not live in vain: If I can ease one life the aching, or cool one pain, or help one fainting robin into his nest again, I shall not live in vain." *Emily Dickinson*

❖ "Everything that I understand, I understand only because I love." *Leo Tolstoy*

Boom Clip

Some years ago, my children were about to do the about to do the World Vision 20 hour famine for the first time. Josiah was eight, Katie seven and Eliza four. They were so excited about it, and I decided to capitalise on this enthusiasm by doing a unit study in our home schooling that month about poverty, compassion and the work of World Vision. Then one night as I drove home from town, I had the idea of using the beautiful allegory of Oscar Wilde's story *The Happy Prince* to help illustrate the importance of learning to be aware of the needs of others. The next morning after devotions, the children helped me write the story into a ten-minute song. We spent the next two months painting the illustrations. It was a wonderful time.

Sometime later we were reading the World Vision magazine and saw an article about a young boy in Wellington who busked on the streets with his violin, and raised enough money each week to enable him to sponsor his own World Vision child.

The children were so inspired by his story and began to think about how they could earn enough money to sponsor their own child. One day as we prayed about it together, we got the idea of publishing the pictures and song in a book with a CD to sell at our concerts. Two years later, this dream became a reality. The book and CD *The Happy Prince* was published and the children chose a beautiful little Zambian girl called Hilda as their sponsored child. (You can check out this book on my web site: *www.boomfamily.co.nz*)

Words To Live By

❖ "This is how we know what love is: Jesus Christ laid down his life for us. And we ought to lay down our lives for our brothers. If anyone has material possessions and sees his brother in need but has no pity on him, how can the love of God be in him? Dear children, let us not love with words or tongue but with actions and in truth." *1 John 4:16-18 NIV*

The Gift of Values

- ❖ "This is what the Lord Almighty says: 'Administer true justice; show mercy and compassion to one another. Do not oppress the widow or the fatherless, the alien or the poor. In your hearts do not think evil of each other.'" *Zechariah 7:9-11 NIV*

- ❖ "True and undefiled religion in the sight of God is this: to visit the orphans and widows in their distress and to keep oneself unstained from the world." *James 1:27 NIV*

- ❖ "Greater love has no one than this, that he lay down his life for his friends." *John 15:13 NIV*

Boom Clip

Some years ago Chris and I attended a friend's wedding. She was marrying a man who had a congenital eye condition and was partially blind. At the reception, his cousin, who had the same eye condition, shared an incident that had happened in her own childhood. She had come home from school one day in tears. When her mother asked her what was the matter, she said that the children had been cruel to her, teasing her and calling her names. Her mother stroked her face and said, "It doesn't matter if you can't see very well with your eyes, darling. What matters most is that you learn to see with your heart."

I was deeply moved by the story. On the long drive home, I composed a song called *Heart*.

Heart

Well, I was just a young'un, barely reached my papa's knees
When my grandma, she said, "I wanna teach you how to see."
So she gathered me up and sat me on her lap
She said, "Listen now, child, with you I want a chat.
You gotta see with your heart, child, and not just with your eyes
Cos there's more to be seen than just the trees and the sky.

You need a heart that's big, not just a head that's smart
No college degree replaces a tender loving heart
What you've gotta seek, what you've gotta find is heart."
Well, the years went by and I learned how to read
I learned to write and do my ABC's
I went to college and I got a degree
But you know, I never forgot the words she said to me
She said, "The Lord, he ain't lookin' for no handsome face
He don't choose the boy that wins a runnin' race.

No, he's looking deeper, yes, deeper to see if He can find
A heart that's big and a heart that's kind.
Intelligence and beauty, they won't hang around
They'll fade like the bushes in the arid ground
What you gotta seek, and what you gotta find, is heart, child, heart.
What you gotta seek, and what you gotta find, is heart.

(You can listen to this song on our web site *www.boomfamily.co.nz*)

Dig Deeper

❖ Watch the DVD *The Hiding Place* with your older children. There are some scenes in it that your younger children would find disturbing.

The Gift of Values

- Watch the DVD *Boenhoeffer* with your older children. It tells the true story of a young German pastor who dared to speak out against Hitler.

- Read *The Diary of Anne Frank*. When Anne is thirteen years old she receives a diary for her birthday. The diary charts all her feelings, hopes and fears during the next two years as she and her family hide from the Nazis.

- Your older children may enjoy reading *Amazing Grace* by Eric Mataxas. It tells the inspiring story of William Wilberforce's tenacity in his fight to abolish the slave trade. Compassion is what motivates him.

- Read *The Happy Prince* by Oscar Wilde. One night a little swallow alights at the feet of the statue of the Happy Prince while on his way to Egypt. The prince asks the swallow to stay with him one night and help him reach out to the poor in the city. The swallow ends up staying with the prince and learns how to see with the eyes of compassion. In the Boom version, your children can listen to the story on the CD while looking at the pictures.

- Watch the DVD *Amazing Grace*. At one point, John Newton tells Wilberforce to "just do it!" Compassion is a God-given gift that motivates us into action.

- We watched a DVD called *The Devil's Arithmetic* by Jane Yolen at a friend's place recently. It was a very moving portrayal of the Holocaust. Great viewing for your teenagers.

- Another wonderful DVD to watch with your older children is *Life is Beautiful*. Apparently when the movie screened privately to some Holocaust survivors, they sat still and silent at the end for a few moments, and then gave a standing ovation.

- Read *The Winged Watchman* by Hilda Van Stockum. The Verhargen family risked their lives many times working in the Dutch Underground during World War Two.

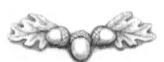

Value Five

PATIENCE

I'm smiling as I begin this chapter. The school holidays have just begun and my children are having fun making a movie, called *The Rescue*. They're all dressed up and at this very moment they're filming the part where the Emperor's guards have come to search the house. Samuel has been instructed to bang loudly on the door and shout, "Open up in the name of the Emperor!" But dear Sam has got all muddled up time and time again, and they are now on the umpteenth 'take.' Chris and I are sitting inside, listening. We can't help smiling at some of the funny mistakes he's made. But my mother's heart has been hoping and praying that the other kids won't get impatient and in frustration ask someone else to do his lines. What a joy to hear Kate and Elle say, "Never mind, Sam! Try again."

A beautiful, timely example to me of the importance of patience. We all cheered when he got it right.

Now, I know this is a value that I need to work on. I often catch myself tapping my fingers on the steering wheel impatiently. And sometimes I feel all wound up inside when I'm running late for something and one of the children isn't ready in time. Perhaps it's those of us who tend to be fast at everything we do that struggle with this the most. I think this was the thing I found hardest when I became a mother. Everything had to slow down. Things took a lot longer - just getting into the car to go to town became a long drawn out process! I found that I needed to slow down - fast - or else I would become extremely uptight and frustrated.

I picked up a book recently at a friend's place, intrigued by the title. It was *In Praise of Slow* by Carl Honore. I read a couple of chapters and could feel myself drinking in the truth of it - slow is beautiful. He decried the 'One Minute Bed time Stories' and reminded us that children long for slow, unhurried stories they can savour.

I read recently in *Word for Today* the advice someone gave to his friend - "you must ruthlessly eliminate hurry from your life."

Fantastic advice. As parents, we spend a lot of time waiting for our children. And we need to exercise even more patience if we home school. Many people have said to me over the years, "Oh, I could never have the patience for home schooling." I promptly tell them that I sure didn't either, but like all the fruit of the Spirit, *it grows*. To be patient, we must relinquish our own agendas, our own timetables. And that's never easy.

Our children will need patience, not only to deal with the inevitable delays of life, but also to deal with unfavourable situations and unfavourable people.

In this chapter, I also want to look at the importance of being patient with ourselves. Last week Chris badly cut two fingers with his drop saw. He had an operation to repair the tendons and stitch the wounds, and is now in a splint for two months. That means no swimming over Christmas, no volleyball, and no house building! He is now enrolled as a student in the school of patience. My twin sister also had an accident this year. She was in hospital for three weeks after her horse fell on her and broke her leg in five places. She is grappling with crutches and the frustration of not being able to do so many things. Illness and physical limitations thrust us into the schoolroom of patience whether we like it or not. We have to learn to be patient with ourselves as well as with others.

And last, but not least, we will also look at the importance of learning to wait. Contrary to what they might tell you, it never hurts your child to have to wait for something. We are not doing them a favour if we always instantly grant them what they want. It is good for them to have to save up or wait for something. Impatience robs us of more things than we ever dream. For example, Kate will never be able to realise her dream of being a piano teacher if she becomes impatient with the preparation that is required. Learning any skill demands patience.

The Bible is full of inspiring stories of men and women who waited patiently for something. Hannah waited for her Samuel; Simeon waited for the Messiah; Joseph waited in Pharaoh's prison for many long years. The Scripture compares our life to a race, and we must run it with patience! Hebrews 6:12 tells us that it is 'through faith and patience we inherit the promises." I've often thought of these two values as the best pair of running shoes I could ever wear as I run my life's race. Faith and Patience.

The Gift of Values

Hannah and the Corn

annah finished sweeping her room and then with a quick glance at the door, she swept the dust and dirt under her bed. *It's not my fault the brush and shovel aren't where they should be,* she muttered to herself.

Anyway, I have far too many chores. Way more than all my friends.

That night at dinner, she fidgeted impatiently in her seat while Mum gave her yet another lecture.

"Hannah, tonight don't be in such a hurry to finish your job. I want you to be more careful when you load the dishwasher. You need to rinse off the dirtiest plates. It just makes it harder for everyone else if you don't."

Hannah felt cross. She was sick of Mum and Dad always going on at her. It seemed like they were always picking on her.

"Okay, Mum," she said as she shoved her chair roughly away from the table. "You don't have to go on about it."

By the time she sat down to do her homework that night, she felt fractious and irritable. She hated math. "Chris!" she called. "Can you help me?" Her brother was a real math geek.

Chris came into her room, chewing on his pencil. "What's up?"

"Can you tell me the answer to this question? It's taking me ages!" Hannah pushed the book over for him to see. Chris sat down by her desk and read the question. Then he grinned at her. "It's easy, Hannah. Here, I'll show you. All you have to understand is how…"

"Oh, for goodness sake, Chris! Just tell me what the answer is. I haven't got time for one of your long drawn-out explanations!"

"But, Hannah," reasoned Chris, "if you just understood how…"

"Oh, give it to me," snapped Hannah as she snatched back her book. "I haven't got time for this." And she turned her back to him and scribbled down an answer.

"Man, you're impatient," muttered Chris as he exited the room. "Haven't you heard that impatience is…" Hannah slammed the door shut.

The next day Hannah woke up with a great feeling. Saturday! No school! She could do whatever she wanted and not have to worry about work.

She went downstairs for breakfast. "Hi, Mum. Okay if I go over to Sharni's house today? We're going to go on a bike ride."

Mum looked at her and smiled. "Sure, honey. But before you go I need you to give me a hand at planting some corn. If we both work at it we'll have it done in a jiffy."

Hannah groaned. "But, Mum! I said I'd be over at nine."

"Well, you'd better give her a call and tell her you'll be a bit later," said Mum. "You know we all have to pitch in and do a few chores on Saturday."

Bother the corn thought Hannah as she trudged outside. *All we seem to do is work around this place.*

Mum got the garden hoe and made a few furrows in the garden. "Come and have a look, Hannah. I'll show you how to do it. You can plant the corn while I do some hoeing."

Mum began dropping the corn seeds in the furrows ten centimetres apart. "Don't plant them too close," she said, "and make sure you cover them well." Then she handed the bag to Hannah.

"I have to plant all these?" said Hannah in disbelief as she looked in the bag. "It'll take forever!"

Mum smiled at her. "No it won't," she said. "Just get stuck in and you'll have it done in no time. We want plenty of corn this year."

But Mum was wrong. It was slow, tedious work. The bag didn't seem to be getting any emptier, and Hannah's back ached. "Aren't you going to help me?" she asked Mum, who was weeding beside her.

"I will in a minute. But first I need to finish this."

Just then the phone rang. Mum put down her hoe and wiped the dirt off her hands. "I'll be back as soon as I can," she said. "Keep at it. And don't be impatient."

The Gift of Values

Hannah glanced at her watch. It was nearly ten o'clock. She looked inside the bag. There were heaps more seeds! It would be lunch time before she got to Sharni's at this rate. Then she had an idea. She glanced at the house. Mum was nowhere to be seen. Hannah made a small hole in the dirt, grabbed a handful of corn seeds and threw a clump of them in. She quickly covered them with the soil and grabbed another handful. The bag soon began to empty. *That's more like it!* thought Hannah.

By the time Mum came back out, Hannah was screwing up the corn bag.

"Are you finished already?" exclaimed Mum. "That was quick!"

"Yep," said Hannah. "I gotta go now. See you just before dinner." And she ran into the shed and found her bike.

She soon forgot all about the corn. The days grew warmer and the garden began to come alive. Tiny plants began appearing everywhere.

Then one morning, Mum came into Hannah's room. She looked serious.

"Hannah, I want you to come with me for a minute."

Hannah followed her mum outside and into the garden area. Suddenly, visions of her corn 'planting' flashed before her eyes. Her mouth went dry and a deep red crept up her neck. Mum said nothing as Hannah looked at the vegetable patch. Tiny corn plants had sprung up in tight bunches all along the rows. Hannah felt the heat rising to her cheeks. There was no hiding it. She'd cheated at the job and everyone knew it.

Mum looked at her with a sad expression on her face. "You can cut corners, Hannah, but it never pays in the end. Soon enough, life has a way of making things very obvious." She watched Hannah's eyes fill with tears.

"I'm sorry, Mum. I truly am."

Mum gazed at her for a moment and then knelt in the dark warm soil. "It's been a good lesson, love, so long as you learn from it. But we're not going to be enjoying much corn this year."

Hannah nodded. What a waste. And it was all her fault. But she'd make sure it never happened again. She got on her knees beside her mother and began pulling out some of the crowded corn plants.

Think About It

- Do you think Hannah was a good worker? Why, or why not?
- What chores did Hannah do sloppily?
- What's wrong with taking short cuts in our work?
- Are the consequences of our actions always obvious immediately?
- Ask the children to think of a time when they became impatient and did something silly.
- Can they think of anyone in the Bible who became impatient and did something they regretted later? (Saul offered the sacrifice when Samuel had expressly told him to wait; Abraham and Sarah took matters into their own hands when they became discouraged waiting for God's promised child; Esau was impatient and wanted a meal 'now.' He traded his birthright for a bowl of soup.)
- What are some of the signs people display when they are impatient? (drumming the fingers; irritability; honking the horn; restlessness)
- This is a question especially for the adults! Can you handle red lights, long queues and delays, or do you quickly become irritated and angry?
- What situation or problem could God be using in your life to build patience?
- Ask your children to think about this question - do you wait until you have enough money to buy something, or do you always want to borrow money?

The Gift of Values

Something To Do

- ❖ If you have the space, plan a vegetable garden with your children. Let them have fun choosing what they'll plant, but make sure you tell them it will need caring for. And that the peas won't be ready in a week!

- ❖ Ask each child to think about a chore that tests their patience. Make sure you share with them about the jobs you have to do that test yours!

- ❖ Design a patience award and present it to the child who has displayed lots of patience. My 'film-makers' have earned their reward today! Maybe I'll surprise them with it tonight at the 'premiere' screening of *The Rescue*.

- ❖ Teach your younger children how to play the card game Patience. (Solitaire)

Boom Clip

I've taken a few 'short cuts' in my life. This particular day, I was fed up with painting windows. How many hours had I spent already, brush in hand, painting in fiddly little places around the window frames? When I reached the last window, and a particularly inaccessible window at that, I saw that I'd missed undercoating part of it. I glanced down at my brush and the can of sage green top coat. The thought of climbing down the ladder, getting the undercoat paint and brush out again, painting the window and then having to wait for it to dry before being able to put on the top coat was just too bothersome. I just wanted to get the job done. I hesitated for a moment as Chris's words rang in my ears - "If we do a really good job of painting the windows, we won't have to paint them again for a long time." Well, I had done a good job so far. But now I just wanted to finish the wretched job. I quickly loaded my brush with the sage green and painted it onto the bare wood. When I'd finished it looked just as good as the other windows! No-one would ever tell the difference.

But I knew. I washed up my brushes with a nagging sense of disappointment in myself. Instead of rejoicing that the huge job of painting all the windows was finished, I was cheated of the satisfaction I should have felt. And when that area of paint started flaking off some time later, I knew it served me right. My 'short cut' turned out to be a 'long cut'. Chris had to sand the window again and I had to get out the undercoat and re-do the job.

So Said

- ❖ "Impatience never commanded success." *Edwin H. Chapin*
- ❖ "Never speak out of anger, never act out of fear; never choose from impatience, but wait… and peace will appear." *Guy Finlay*
- ❖ "It's not that I'm so smart, it's just that I stay with problems longer." *Albert Einstein*
- ❖ "Our patience will achieve more than our force." *Edmund Burke*
- ❖ "Patience wears away stones." *English Proverb*
- ❖ "Patience is counting down without blasting off." *Anon*
- ❖ "Little drops of water wear down big stones." *Russian Proverb*
- ❖ "Patience is the ability to idle your motor when you feel like stripping your gears." *Barbara Johnson*
- ❖ "The key to everything is patience. You get the chicken by hatching the egg - not by smashing it." *Arnold Glasow*
- ❖ "Rome was not built in a day." *Proverb*
- ❖ "If you add a little to a little, and then do it again, soon that little shall be much." *Hesiod*

The Gift of Values

- "Patience is a root of all the goods, mother of piety, fruit that never withers, a fortress that is never taken, a harbor that know no storms." *Chryostrom*
- "Divine patience is not passivity. It is deliberate restraint." *Anon*
- "Patience is coolness under pressure." *Anon*
- "He that can have patience, can have what he will." *Benjamin Franklin*

Words To Live By

- "Be patient, then, brothers, until the Lord's coming. See how the farmer waits for the land to yield its valuable crop and how patient he is for the autumn and spring rains." *James 5:7 NIV*
- "A man's wisdom gives him patience." *Proverbs 19:11 NIV*
- "We do not want you to become lazy, but to imitate those who through faith and patience inherit what has been promised." *Hebrews 6:12 NIV*
- "Whatever you do, work at it with all your heart, as working for the Lord and not for men." *Colossians 3:23 NIV*

Dig Deeper

- Read *The Carrot Seed* by Ruth Krauss with your younger children. A little boy plants a carrot seed. Then he waters, weeds and waits, until one glorious day, the carrot is ready.
- Read *Hans Brinker* or *The Silver Skates* by Mary Dodge. This classic story showcases many values - honour, compassion, diligence, faith and patience.

Patience

- ❖ Read the French tale, *The Magic Thread*. (You can Google search it and read it online.) Peter is given a ball of thread by an old woman.

"This is your life thread," she told him. "Do not touch it and time will pass normally. But if you wish time to pass more quickly, you have only to pull the thread a little way and an hour will pass like a second. But I warn you, once the thread has been pulled out, it cannot be pushed back in again. It will disappear like a puff of smoke. The ball is for you. But if you accept my gift you must tell no one, or on that very day you shall die. Now, say, do you want it?"

Too often, people want what they want, or what they think they want, right now. The irony of their impatience is that usually only by learning to wait, and by a willingness to accept the bad with the good, do we attain those things that are truly worthwhile.

The Gift of Values

Uncle Hendrik's Moustache

ncle Hendrik looked at his two nephews, and a gleam came to his eye. This was his chance to teach the bothersome little boys a lesson. He stroked his black bushy moustache and wriggled his thick eyebrows.

"So you want to grow a moustache like mine, eh?"

The two boys nodded their heads furiously and waited in excited silence.

"Follow me," said Uncle Hendrik and strode out the door. The two boys scampered after him, barely able to contain their excitement. At last they would each have a moustache they could twirl and stroke like Uncle Hendrik's.

He took them out the back of the house to a large bunion tree where chickens and roosters scratched and pecked.

"Right," he said, "sit down."

They sat on the dry ground and looked up at him with eager faces.

Uncle Hendrik looked at them with a hint of a smile and said, "Now you must keep this on for a long time or it won't work." And he scooped up some chicken dung on his finger and plastered it on their top lip. Their noses wrinkled up and they closed their eyes. It smelt terrible. But they weren't going to wipe it off. No, they were going to grow two fine bushy moustaches no matter what.

Uncle Hendrik glanced back at the two little figures huddled under the tree and saw the look of grim determination on their faces. He chuckled and stroked his fine moustache and gave it another twirl.

Think About It

- Will the boys ever grow their moustaches this way? How long will they have to sit there?

- Ask your children to think of other things that take time to grow. Trees; plants; hair; fingernails; children; babies. Point out to them that growing a child in the womb has a God-appointed time of nine months. If it is born long before it is due, a baby cannot survive. There is an appointed time for everything - even growing moustaches! Impatience never gives us the result we want.

- Ask your children to think of things which require patience to learn. I once nursed a man who had had his left big toe cut off. He had to learn how to walk again. I remember how impatient he used to get when he lost his balance.

Something To Do

- Have some fun making false moustaches. My children sported some great painted ones the other night, for a play they put on. You could coin a saying to go with the moustaches. What about 'Some things take time'?

- Read together *Ecclesiastes 3:1-11*. Help the children make a cardboard clock and decorate it with the verse, 'There is a time for everything'.

- Play some board games together. Choose ones that have a timer, and after the game discuss whether they would like to always be racing against a clock like that.

- Get a book out of the library which illustrates the growth of a baby in the womb.

The Gift of Values

- Ask the children what they think the following Chinese proverb means. *"Patience is power; with time and patience the mulberry leaf becomes a silk gown."*

Research about the amazing work of silkworms. The story of silk begins in China. Have a child find China on a world map. A silkworm's cocoon is made of one strand of silk as long as a half a mile long. Strands are then twisted together into threads. Machines weave them into beautiful silk cloth, famous for its strength, texture and light weight. It takes thousands of cocoons to make one bolt of silk. The wedding gown for Diana, the former Princess of Wales, was made from 165 yards of silk!

Read *The Empress and the Silkworm* by Lily Joy Hong with your younger children. When a cocoon from a mulberry tree falls into Si Ling-Chi's hot cup of tea, the tightly wound cocoon start to unravel. She plucks it out and finds it is made of a fine, shimmering thread. The empress realises that these shining strands spun by tiny worms could be woven into a fabric almost magical in its beauty. But it takes time and patience.

So Said...

- "The trees that are slow to grow bear the best fruit." *Moliere*
- "Patience is emotional diligence. It reveals love. It gives birth to understanding." *Steven R. Covey*
- "If you are patient in one moment of anger, you will escape a hundred days of sorrow." *Chinese Proverb*
- "Patience and tenacity of purpose are worth more than twice their weight of cleverness." *Thomas Henry Huxley*
- "There is more to life than increasing its speed." *Ghandi*
- "All of nature is a lesson in patience." *Anon*

- "Beware the fury of a patient man." *John Dryden*

- "Impatience is the worst of thieves." *R.J.Boom*

- "Adopt the pace of nature: her secret is patience." *Ralph Waldo Emerson*

- "Quiet waiting before God would save from many a mistake and from many a sorrow." *J. Hudson Taylor*

- "Even the richest soil, if left uncultivated will produce the rankest weeds." *Leonardo da Vinci*

- "Our patience will achieve more than our force." *Edmund Burke*

- "Patience is the companion of wisdom." *St Augustine*

- "Persevere without patience, you will probably succeed, but you will be frequently frustrated. If you are patient without perseverance, you will probably be comfortable, but never achieve your objectives. The key is to keep yourself in balance by developing both qualities at the same time." *Anon*

- "The faster you go, the easier it is to get lost." *Anon*

- "One of the greatest virtues anyone can possess is the ability to wait." *Anon*

The Gift of Values

Boom Clip

When I was involved in missionary work in Borneo, I was given a certain sum of money from my church back home in New Zealand, designated to be used solely for myself. So the next time I was able to visit a Christian book store, I spent several happy hours searching for a good book. I walked out of the shop with *The Letters of Samuel Rutherford*. What a blessing that book was to me. Rutherford was a pastor in the 17th century in Scotland. He was sent into exile for many years, and over that time wrote many God-inspired letters to different members of his congregation. One in particular touched me deeply. It was written to a woman who had lost a child and was desperate to conceive again.

"Madam, do not prig [complain, argue, contend] with our gracious and loving Lord about the time of the fulfilling of your joys. It will be, God has said it. Bide His time, wait His harvest. His day is better than your day. *It is not for us to set an hourglass to the Creator of Time.*"

That last sentence made a powerful impression on me. At the time of reading it, I was a single girl, thirty years old, and longing to be married. I knew only too well how easy it was to set an hourglass to the Creator of Time. How many times had I said to God, "Please, Lord! I need You to bring my husband to me before I go to the mission field... before I turn twenty five... before I turn thirty..."?

I remember turning over an 'hourglass' (a two-minute timer for a board game) and realising that I had done that so many times in my life to God... "Right, Lord, You've got two months; three weeks; a year..." And this to the Creator of Time!

Words To Live By

❖ "Be imitators of those who through faith and patience inherit the promise." *Hebrews 6:12 NIV*

Patience

- My brethren, count it all joy when you fall into various trials, knowing that the testing of your faith produces patience. But let patience have its perfect work, that you may be perfect and complete, lacking nothing. *James 1:4 NKJV*

- "Love is patient and kind..." *1 Corinthians 13:1NIV*

- "Therefore, as God's chosen people, holy and dearly loved, clothe yourselves with compassion, kindness, humility, gentleness and patience." *Colossians 3:12 NIV*

- "When the people saw that Moses was so long in coming down from the mountain, they gathered around Aaron and said, 'Come, make us gods who will go before us. As for this fellow Moses who brought us up out of Egypt, we don't know what has happened to him.'" *Exodus 32:1 NIV*

Dig Deeper

- Read *Where the Red Fern Grows* by Wilson Rawls. Billy yearns for two coon hounds, but his parents are poor and can't afford them. Billy patiently works and saves enough money to buy them himself. This beautiful story is also available on DVD.

- Read about Anne Sullivan, Helen Keller's teacher. She is a magnificent example of patience. Without her patience, the world would never have known and loved Helen Keller.

- Read *The Magic Fishbone* by Charles Dickens. Alicia's impatient father learns some very important lessons.

- Read *The Diary of Remember Patience Whipple* by Kathryn Lasky. This is the journal of a fun-loving girl named Remember who tries very hard to live up to her middle name, 'Patience.' She calls herself 'Imp' for short. (Short for Impatience!)

The Gift of Values

Show Me How To Live

"We'll have to train new muscles to do the work of old ones," said the physiotherapist as she strapped Joni's arms into special slings. "It's not going to be easy, but you can do it." Joni gritted her teeth and closed her eyes. Nothing was easy these days. Why did she have to fight so hard for every little thing, when all her friends could walk and move by themselves? She hated having to let a nurse brush her teeth. And brush her hair. And wipe her nose.

"Okay, Joni," said the therapist cheerfully. "Let's give it a try."

For the next ten minutes Joni tried to lift her arms off the bed. Finally she lay still, feeling exhausted and angry. It was no good. She was trapped inside her useless body, feeling angry at everyone.

"C'mon, Joni. Try again!" urged the therapist.

Joni's eyes snapped open. "Don't you think I'm trying?" she shouted. "Just leave me alone."

The therapist looked at Joni and gave her an understanding smile. "It's alright, Joni. Take a break for a few minutes. We'll have another go when you're ready."

Angry feelings churned inside Joni as she turned her head away from the therapist and closed her eyes. She remembered the accident as if it was just yesterday. And the panic she'd felt as she lay face down in the water, un-able to breathe, and un-able to lift her head. Those few seconds had changed her life forever. If only she had checked the water. If only she hadn't dived in. Now, five months later, the same feeling of panic overwhelmed her again. Except instead of drowning in water, she was drowning in frustration and helplessness. She lay there for a few minutes, trying to bring her feelings under control. "God, help me!" she prayed silently.

The prayer had scarcely left her heart when she remembered something that had happened the other day. Her friend, Dick, had discovered a verse in James and read it out to her. "Is your life full of difficulties and temptations?

Then be happy, for when the way is rough, your patience has a chance to grow."

Something had happened inside her when she'd heard that verse. She knew she had a choice. Life sure was rough. Since the accident, she'd begged God over and over again to let her die. But that day, after hearing the verse, she had changed her prayer. "Lord, if I can't die, show me how to live."

Joni gave a wry smile and stared up at the white ceiling. *Well, if I'm going to live, one thing's for sure. I'm going to need a lot of patience.*

"I'm ready to try again," she said, turning her head.

The physiotherapist gave her the thumbs up. "Way to go, Joni!"

This time when she tried, Joni managed to lift her arms a full inch off the bed.

Over the next year, Joni's patience had countless chances to grow. Learning to drive her electric wheelchair wasn't easy. She spent two hours coaxing it thirty feet along the corridor. Then when she veered into the wall and got stuck, she had to sit and wait for half an hour for someone to come and help her. Later, she spent long, tiring hours learning to hold a pen in her mouth. It took a lot of patience before she could finally write her name. And when the paintbrush slopped paint everywhere and ruined her picture, she learnt to be patient with herself and try again. Life wasn't easy, but eventually patience brought her many rewards. Joni became a successful artist, author, singer and public speaker. Patience had become an essential, vital part of her everyday life and experience. But her life of suffering and patient overcoming became the source of encouragement and inspiration to many people across the world.

"Living in a wheelchair is not easy," says Joni. "But this wheelchair has been my passport to places I could never have reached without it. Now I thank God for my wheelchair."

The Gift of Values

Think About It

- ❖ How did Joni's accident happen?
- ❖ What does the word 'quadriplegic' mean?
- ❖ Name some of the things that Joni had to learn to do.
- ❖ What was the prayer Joni prayed that became the turning point in her life?
- ❖ Joni has spent forty years in her wheelchair. Do you think she still needs patience?
- ❖ How would you feel if you had to wait for someone to get you out of bed in the morning, dress you and feed you?
- ❖ Do you think it would easy to become grumpy and impatient with the people who are trying to help you?
- ❖ Why does Joni thank God for her wheelchair?

Something To Do

- ❖ Get your children to try writing their name by holding a pen in their mouth. (Try it yourself!) The older children could also try painting a picture. Make sure they decide what they're going to paint first, so they can't quit when the first niggles of impatience begin to appear!
- ❖ Discuss with your older children some of the physical challenges people face. Perhaps a grandparent has suffered a stroke? Discuss the frustrations they may have to cope with.
- ❖ Do a research project together on spinal injuries.
- ❖ Get your older children to wear an arm in a sling for a day. Just getting dressed, brushing teeth and making their bed will become a real challenge. It will make them realise how much we need to develop patience.

Boom Clip

One winter, when the children were young, Chris and I sat together each evening by the fire and read Corrie ten Boom's book, *A Prisoner and Yet*. I found one part deeply moving. Corrie's mother suffered a stroke one day, and from that time on, she could only say three words - no, yes and Corrie. It must have been such a frustration for her, but Corrie said that her mother cheerfully played a necessary game for them to know what she was thinking or feeling. They would sit her by the window, where she could look out on her beloved street in Haarlem.

"Corrie," she would say.

"What is it, Mother? Did you see someone?"

"Yes!"

"Was it an old friend?"

"Yes!"

"Was it a man?"

"No."

"Was it so and so?"

"Yes!"

"Mama, I'll bet it's her birthday!"

"YES!"

Once the mystery was solved, Corrie would then write a note to the person, saying that her mother had seen her from the window, and remembered it was her birthday. Then Corrie would put the pen in her mother's stiffened fingers and Mrs. ten Boom would sign the letter with a shaky cross, which soon became the most loved signature in Haarlem.

What a beautiful example of the need for patience, and its wonderful reward.

So Said...

- ❖ "Patience makes lighter what sorrow may not heal." *Horace*

- ❖ "Patience is waiting. Not passively waiting. That is laziness. But to keep going when the going is hard and slow - that is patience." *Anon*

- ❖ "Have patience with all things, but mostly with yourself."
  St. Francis de Sales

- ❖ "He who would learn to fly must first learn to walk and run and climb and dance; one cannot fly into flying." *Nietzsche*

- ❖ "Patience can't be acquired overnight. It is just like building up a muscle. Every day you need to work on it." *Eknath Easwaran*

- ❖ "It turns out having no arms and legs has gotten me into some doors I would not have been able to walk through." *Nick Vujicic*

- ❖ "We could never learn to be brave and patient, if there were only joy in the world." *Helen Keller*

Boom Clip

I remember the day I visited the McKean Leprosy Hospital in Thailand. I met a man who was painstakingly carving a small piece of teak wood. His hands were stumps, and a slender chisel was strapped to the knuckle joint of his missing first finger. I watched, mesmerised, as the thin shavings of wood fell to the dirt floor. I turned to my guide.

"Would you please ask him what he's making?"

My interpreter posed the question, and immediately the woodcarver beamed at me and beckoned me closer. He reached beneath the bench and pulled out the most exquisite carving I had ever seen. A girl, with eyes closed, kneeling into the open hand of God. I turned it over in my hands, not wanting to let it go. I looked at the deformed face of the carver, whose brown eyes were still smiling at me.

Patience

"It's beautiful," I told him.

When he offered it to me, I willingly emptied my purse and gave him all its contents. That carving was the most precious purchase I made during my whole time in Asia.

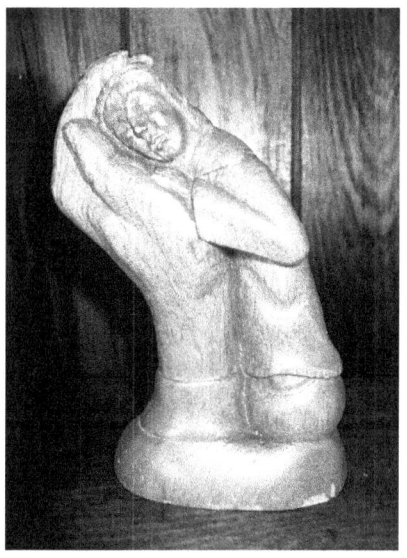

Words To Live By

❖ "Rather, as servants of God we commend ourselves in every way: in great endurance; in troubles; hardships and distresses; in beatings, imprisonments and riots; in hard work, sleepless nights and hunger; in purity, understanding, patience and kindness…" *2 Corinthians 6:4-6 NIV*

❖ "Brothers, as an example of patience in the face of suffering, take the prophets who spoke in the name of the Lord. As you know, we consider blessed those who have persevered. You have heard of Job's perseverance and have seen what the Lord finally brought about. The Lord is full of compassion and mercy." *James 5:10,11 NIV*

The Gift of Values

- "And so after waiting patiently, Abraham received what was promised." Hebrews 6:15 NIV

Dig Deeper

- Go to *www.LifeWithoutLimbs.org* and read the inspiring story of Nick Vujicic, a young Australian man who was born without arms and legs. Nick has faced countless challenges, but has become an inspiring communicator, sharing his faith and love of God to people all over the world. There are a number of videos on his site, where you can watch him brush his hair, shave and swim. You can hear him preach and share about his life. Inspiring stuff! He has a new DVD *Life's Greater Purpose* which you can order on his web site. He has also written a book called *No Arms, No Legs, No worries.*

- Read one of the many books about Joni Earekson Tada. Your local library is bound to have at least one of them.

- Your older children could read *Picking up the Pieces* by Patricia Calvert. Megan becomes paralyzed in a motorbike accident. The book offers a perceptive and honest look at the struggles she faces, and tells how she finally learns to accept the devastating changes that are forced upon her, and begins to look ahead with hope.

Value Six

FORGIVENESS

I woke up at 3am today and lay in bed, listening to the pouring rain on the tin roof of our barn and thinking about forgiveness. Imagine a world without forgiveness. There would be no lasting relationships, no happy marriages, and no successful families. Hurts are unavoidable and come all too often. Our hearts can so easily become wounded and angry. There is only one way we can ever know complete healing and restoration of broken relationships - that is with true forgiveness.

Katherine Porter once said, "Love must be learned, and learned again and again; hate needs no instruction, but waits only to be provoked."

I think that love and forgiveness are so closely entwined that it is almost impossible to discern one from the other. And in the same way that love must be learned, forgiveness must be learned also. We must learn how to ask for forgiveness when we have wronged someone, and we must learn how to forgive someone who has wronged us. This will be one of the most important things our children ever learn. And what better place to learn forgiveness than in a family? The opportunities to forgive come daily.

As parents, we need to model forgiveness for our children. It's not enough to talk about it, we must live it. We need to freely and whole-heartedly forgive our children when they hurt us. And in the same way, we must ask for their forgiveness each time we hurt them. Every parent makes mistakes. Just yesterday, I went out to the washing line and saw our young puppy, Lucy, standing beside a dead hen. I was horrified.

The Gift of Values

I knew I had to teach her a lesson before she became a confirmed chicken-killer, so I gave Lucy a sound scolding and she slunk off. Only then did I notice the hen had its eyes open. I looked again and realised that there was no blood on it anywhere. Seconds later, the hen got up and began walking around. I felt terrible. For all I know, Lucy may have just seen the hen out on the lawn and been sniffing it. It made me remember other times when I've jumped to conclusions and dealt out unjust punishments to my children. I am slowly learning not to make hasty judgements and to wait until I've heard both sides of the story. But I still make mistakes. However, when I apologise and ask for forgiveness, it becomes a powerful example of how to act when we wrong someone.

In her book, *Easing the Pain of Parenthood*, Mary Rae Deatrick says, "I beseech you not to think of failure as final. If you have previously blown it with your child by speaking heart-damaging words, express your grief to him or her and ask their forgiveness. Turn the tables on failure by walking in words of forgiveness and love. There are hundreds of words to choose from. Take your pick. For myself, I am particularly fond of *forgive* and *love* and *care* and *appreciate* and *respect* and *need*. They team especially well with *I* and *you*."

We must teach our children *how* to forgive, *whom* to forgive and *when* to forgive. We've probably all seen the look on the face of a child when we've told them to apologise to their little brother for hitting him on the head. And we've all heard the many different ways a child can mumble the words, "I'm sorry", while making it very clear they are anything but sorry. Forgiveness isn't grumbling or spitting out a couple of magic words. We need to teach our children how to forgive from the heart, and that they can *choose* to forgive even when they don't feel like it. They need to know *why* they should forgive, and what a difference it will make in their relationships and in their life if they do. Jesus taught His disciples so much about forgiveness. He knew that it didn't come naturally or easily.

I hope this chapter will help shine the spotlight on forgiveness, and help our children (and us) learn how to offer forgiveness freely and also how to receive it. As we do, we will discover it is one of God's most precious gifts.

Hard Choices

ymkhana morning! I leapt out of bed, and went to wake up my twin sister, Penny. I'd barely slept that night, waiting for my alarm to go off. After a quick breakfast, we set off on our bikes along the dark, empty streets. It was only 5.30 am but we had a lot to do. We needed to groom our ponies, plait their manes and tails, put on their leg bandages and be ready for the truck at 7.00 am.

"Gypsy! Here, girl!" I was bursting with excitement as I called out to my skewbald pony. I peered through the drifts of morning mist as she appeared, nickering softly.

"Rose!" My sister's voice was sharp. "Look!"

We stared in disbelief as Gypsy reached us.

"No!" I wailed.

Gypsy's beautiful mane and tail had been hacked off. Crude lumps of mane stuck out along her neck. All that was left of her tail was a few patches of short hair along the bony stump.

Gypsy nuzzled at my pockets, searching for a treat. Her breath was warm on my hands. Rage welled up inside me. "Who would do such a thing?!' I stormed. "Who could be so cruel?"

There would be no gymkhana for me that day.

Mum and Dad were just getting up when we returned home. I tried to tell them what had happened but my throat choked up and no words came. Penny told them what had happened. When Mum looked at me sadly, I finally found my voice.

"I hate them!' I shouted. "I hate whoever did this!"

"Darling!" said Mum. "You mustn't say that. Gypsy's mane and tail will grow again."

"But you don't understand! It'll take months!" I ran out of the room and slammed the door.

The next day was awful. I had never felt so much anger before. All I could think about was revenge. Every time I remembered my beautiful pony with her ragged mane and tail, my stomach churned and a bitter taste filled my mouth. I couldn't eat my lunch.

"What if whoever did it attacks my pony tonight?" asked Penny as we walked home from church. "Are we just going to sit around and do nothing?"

"No way!" I said. "Here's what we'll do."

That night, we sat crouched in our hideout behind the oak trees, wriggling our toes to try and bring back some feeling. It had been two hours since we'd set up position in the bushes, but it seemed like five. The moon threw a silver sheen on the rumps of our two ponies quietly grazing in the paddock. A mosquito buzzed near my ear. I slapped my face and the buzzing stopped.

"Sshh," whispered Penny.

A figure was climbing over the post and rail fence. I froze. I could feel my heart pounding as if it would jump out of my chest. The shape half ran, half walked along the fence line, then out into the paddock. I tightened my grip on the spotlight.

"Not yet," whispered Penny. "Wait."

Penny's bay pony, Fleet, nickered softly and turned towards the person's outstretched hand. His beautiful black mane looked almost blue in the moonlight.

"Steady." I said it as much to myself as to my sister.

Something else glinted in the moonlight.

"Now!"

Whooping and yelling, we leapt from the bushes. The stark glare of my spotlight trapped a figure in its beam.

"Sophie!" gasped Penny.

Forgiveness

I stared in unbelief. But there was no mistaking it. Sophie Liddicoat spun around and stared at us, her eyes wide with fright. Then she bolted like a hare before the hounds. I kept the beam of the flashlight on her as long as I could.

"Run!" I screamed after her. "Run, you miserable beast!" It felt good to let the rage out.

"So! Sophie Liddicoat," said Penny when she had disappeared from sight. "I would never have thought she'd stoop as low as this."

Sophie Liddicoat was in our class at school. Nobody liked her. But then, Sophie didn't exactly make it easy for people to like her. I'd had a run-in with her at school just the other day. I'd teased her about something - it was only a joke - but Sophie had got really angry, and lashed out with some pretty mean words of her own. I'd felt sorry about it later, but there was no way I was going to apologise to Sophie.

I went straight to bed when we got home. I didn't want to talk to anybody. Penny must have told Mum what had happened, because soon there was a soft knock on my door. Mum came in and sat on the bed. I pretended I was asleep, but she knew better.

"Rose, darling, we need to talk."

I made a noise, but didn't sit up. Mum gently rubbed my shoulders. They were stiff and tense.

"It's awful what Sophie did, honey, but you need to forgive her. If you don't, you'll just feel miserable."

"That's easy for you to say!" I mumbled. The anger tumbled around inside, and made it hard even to talk.

"Let it go, Rose. Let go of your anger. There's nothing worse than having it eating away inside."

"But I can't stop hating her, Mum!"

"Yes, you can," she said. "All you have to do is choose to forgive her. God will take away the hate, if you let Him."

I lay there, trying to relax. Mum's fingers massaged my neck and shoulders, and I knew she was praying.

"All right," I said finally. "I'll try."

"Good girl!" said Mum. "You'll feel a whole lot better as soon as you pray. I know. I've had to forgive people before, too." She gave me a kiss and left the room.

I sat up in bed and put my head on my knees. I didn't really know how to start. Part of me wanted to pray, but another part of me wanted to keep hating Sophie. Finally I made a choice.

"Dear Lord, please help me. I've got so much hate inside and I can't stop thinking awful things about Sophie. But I want to stop. I want to forgive her for doing that to Gypsy."

I was meaning to say a lot more, but at that moment a warm wave of love washed through my heart. It swallowed up my anger and hate, and left in their place a peace that I'd never felt before. I felt light, as if a huge weight had rolled off me. It was like waking up after a nightmare and realising that it had only been a dream. I laughed out loud.

Suddenly I felt hungry. It had been ages since I'd been able to eat anything. I jumped out of bed and went to the kitchen, a big smile on my face. As I put the bread in the toaster, I made another decision. The next day at school, I'd find Sophie and ask her to forgive me for all the mean things I'd said to her. If she could just feel the joy I was feeling now.

Who knows, we might even end up friends.

Think About It

❖ Why do you think Sophie cut off Gypsy's tail?

❖ How do you feel inside when you're angry with someone?

❖ Is forgiveness a choice?

❖ Do we wait until someone says sorry before we forgive? What if they are never sorry? Get one of the children to find the verse in the Bible that tells us that 'while we were still sinners, Christ died for us.'

Something To Do

❖ Discuss what to say if you've wronged someone. Is 'I'm sorry' enough? When we have said something unkind, how should we apologise? - "I'm so sorry I said that. I know I've hurt you with my words. Please forgive me."

A note to parents here - how often have we let our children down by forgetting or failing to keep our promises? If we have, it's important that we apologise to our children rather than make excuses. Perhaps our son has told us that we never listen to him properly - that we always interrupt. We need to ask for forgiveness, but then also work hard at not committing the same offence again.

❖ Do some role-plays with your children. Think up age-appropriate scenarios. For example: If Jonny has just eaten Suzie's chocolate bar that she'd hidden in the fridge, what should he say? ("I'm sorry I ate your chocolate bar, Suzie. Will you forgive me?")

❖ Discuss what Jonny should do next. Should he offer to buy her a new chocolate bar?

❖ Explain to your children that every time they choose to be kind, or forgive, or say something encouraging to someone, it's like depositing a sum of money into that person's emotional bank account. Likewise, every time they are mean, or say something hurtful for example, they make a withdrawal from that person's emotional bank account. Get your children to draw up two lists - one for deposits, one for withdrawals.

The Gift of Values

Some ideas we had:

- ❖ **Deposits**
    - Sharing toys
    - Saying thank you
    - Helping each other
    - Playing together
    - Apologising
    - Forgiving when someone says 'I'm sorry.'
    - Saying 'I love you.'
    - Keeping a promise…

- ❖ **Withdrawals**
    - Ignoring someone
    - Hitting, punching, pushing
    - Not sharing
    - Not saying thank you
    - Refusing to apologise, or doing it insincerely
    - Not playing together
    - Not keeping a promise…

You can make up as many as you like. One of the most exciting aspects about this is that we can proactively turn any family problem or issue into an opportunity to make a deposit. For example, if Sam gets angry and hits Jacob, Jacob has the opportunity to make a huge deposit in the bank by forgiving him. If Josiah wakes up grumpy and tired and snaps at Milly, there is the opportunity for her to make a large deposit into his bank account by being kind to him.

The important thing is that the children will soon realise that most of our actions and words either make a deposit into, or a withdrawal from, someone's emotional bank account.

In a family, we want everyone's emotional bank balance to be in the black, fat and healthy! That way, when hard times come, there is a good reserve that can handle some of life's unavoidable 'withdrawals.'

Forgiveness

- ❖ Play *'The Piggybank Game'* with your younger children. Buy a cheap piggybank and set aside a supply of coins. Explain to the children that whatever is in the piggybank at the end of the day or week, the family can have fun spending on something together. Then tell them that every time they are kind, or forgiving, they can get a coin and put it in the piggybank. But if they are unkind, or hit and fight, they must take out a coin and return it to the money jar. At the end of the day, count out how much money there is. They will quickly understand that all their actions make a difference.

- ❖ Read together *Psalm 32*. It is the joyful proclamation of the happy state of those who experience God's forgiveness. David was troubled and miserable when he tried to hide his sin, but full confession brought wonderful relief. Discuss David's sin. You could also read *Psalm 51* together.

- ❖ Memorise together the poem, *The Quarrel* by Eleanor Farjeon.

> *I quarrelled with my brother,*
> *I don't know what about,*
> *One thing led to another*
> *And somehow we fell out.*
> *The start of it was slight,*
> *The end of it was strong,*
> *He said he was right,*
> *I knew he was wrong!*
>
> *We hated one another.*
> *The afternoon turned black.*
> *Then suddenly my brother*
> *Thumped me on my back,*
> *And said, "Oh, come along!*
> *We can't go on all night -*
> *I was in the wrong."*
> *So he was in the right*

The Gift of Values

- Read together *Matthew 18:23-35*. This parable is a great one to act out. Through this parable, Jesus teaches us about our relationship to God:

    God, our King, cancels our debts because
    He is a forgiving and loving God.

    The debt of our sin against God is so enormous
    we can never hope to repay it.

    The sins which others commit against us are small
    and insignificant compared to the debt we owe our master.

    It is in our fallen human nature to withhold forgiveness.

    When we refuse to forgive others,
    we block God's flow of forgiveness towards us.

Boom Clip

We had just read the story of the unforgiving servant in Matthew chapter 18. We decided to act it out in an impromptu play. Josiah pushed the paper crown back on his head and tried not to laugh as Eliza threw herself at his feet and begged for mercy and more time to pay off her huge debt.

I was videoing the drama and trying hard not to chuckle at the impromptu wording and actions. But I couldn't help it when Eliza fell upon her hapless little brother Jacob who owed her a mere two dollars. As she took him by the throat and proceeded to choke him, (it was in the Bible passage!) he squeaked out, "Mercy!" It sounded so small, so pathetic. We all burst out laughing. Then Eliza was dragged before the King again, kicking and yelling, and both our dogs joined in the fracas - total chaos and bedlam, but we'll never forget that parable!

So Said...

- "The grandest expression of love is to forgive. It is our most unselfish act and therefore the most difficult and most rewarding." *Richard. P Walters*

- "Daily relationships make forgiveness an often repeated necessity, without limits." *Anon*

- "As long as we love, we can forgive." *La Rochefoucauld.*

- "Let us correct what we can correct, change what we can change, and forgive all the mess that is left over." *Mary Rae Deatrick*

- "If you're going to bow, bow low." *Eastern proverb*

- "The weak can never forgive. Forgiveness is the attribute of the strong." *Mahatma Gandhi*

- "Most of us can forgive and forget; we just don't want the other person to forget that we forgave." *Ivern Ball*

- "Forgive or relive." *Anon*

- To carry a grudge is like being stung to death by one bee." *William H. Walton*

- "He that cannot forgive others, breaks the bridge over which he himself must pass if he would ever reach heaven; for everyone has need to be forgiven." *George Herbert*

- "Without forgiveness, there's no future." *Desmond Tutu*

- "The difference between holding on to a hurt or releasing it with forgiveness is like the difference between laying your head down at night on a pillow filled with thorns or a pillow filled with rose petals." *Loren Fischer*

- "Life is an adventure in forgiveness." *Norman Cousins*

The Gift of Values

- "Forgiveness is me giving up my right to hurt you for hurting me."
  Anon

- "Forgiveness is not an occasional act: it is a permanent attitude."
  Dr. Martin Luther King

Boom Clip

I remember in my own childhood a time when one of the children greatly annoyed and upset one of their siblings. When the guilty party came and apologised for upsetting him, he spat back at her, "You still did it!"

When God forgives, He never answers like that!

Words To Live By

- "Be kind and compassionate to one another, forgiving one another, just as in Christ God forgave you." *Ephesians 4:32 NIV*

- "Then Peter came to Jesus and asked, 'Lord, how many times shall I forgive my brother when he sins against me? Up to seven times?' Jesus answered, 'I tell you, not seven times, but seventy-seven times.'" *Matthew 18:21,22 NIV*

- "And when you stand praying, if you hold anything against anyone, forgive him, so that your Father in heaven may forgive you your sins." *Mark 11:25 NIV*

- "Bear with each other and forgive whatever grievances you may have against one another. Forgive as the Lord forgave you." *Colossians 3:13 NIV*

- "He who covers a transgression, seeks love." *Proverbs 17:9 NASB*

- "Above all keep fervent in your love for one another, because love covers a multitude of sins." *1 Peter 4:8 NASB*

Dig Deeper

- Mums and dads, read *How to Forgive Your Children* by Quin Sherrer. It is a challenging and inspirational book filled with true stories that illustrate the power of forgiveness.

- Watch the movie *Les Miserables* with your older children. Jean Valjean's life is turned around when he is forgiven by the priest he attacked and robbed. Javert, his former jailer and later a policeman, knows only an unforgiving, unyielding form of justice. As I watched this movie, I kept thinking of the verse that says, 'For judgment will be merciless to one who has shown no mercy; mercy triumphs over judgment." *James 2:13 NASB*

- There are some wonderful moments in *Anne of Green Gables* by L. Montgomery where Anne has to apologise for mistakes she has made. It also showcases the unforgiveness she harbours against Gilbert Blythe for calling her 'Carrots.' Marilla also confesses to Anne that she once held an unforgiving attitude against Gilbert's father, and thought she could punish him by not forgiving him. Yet now, she wishes she had forgiven him years before.

- Watch the DVD *Shrek*. Listen out for Donkey's famous line, "That's what friends do! They forgive each other!"

- A great book for parents to read is *The Key to Your Child's Heart* by Gary Smalley. I learned a lot from this book. How do you ensure your child's heart remains open and loving towards you? Read this book!

- Watch the DVD *Treasures of the Snow* by Patricia St. John, or read the book. Annette's little brother has a terrible accident and is crippled when teased by the village bully, Lucien. Annette hates Lucien vehemently after the accident, but must come to terms with her bitterness and hatred. It's a great story of forgiveness.

The Gift of Values

- Read *The Lion, the Witch and the Wardrobe* by C. S. Lewis or watch the DVD. Peter, Susan and Lucy must forgive their brother, Edmund for betraying them to the White Witch.

- Watch the *Little Dogs on the Prairie* video called *Pride, Prejudice and Fudge*. It shows the folly of carrying a grudge.

- Our family has loved reading *The Viking Quest* series by Lois Walfrid Johnson. Viking raiders take young Bree and Devin O'Toole and other Irish people from their homes as slaves. In the second book Devin battles with the hatred he feels for the Vikings, and finally comes to a place where he chooses to forgive. Fabulous read aloud books, with a great message and lots of adventure!

☙

The Shepherd's Call

ngry lightning scratched across the black sky. Two figures made their way across the moor, hunched against the driving rain. One was just a child, the other a large man. Every few steps, the man cupped his hands around his mouth, and rang out a call, clear and strong, and the wind caught it and tossed it around, before flinging it to the ground. Then the man and the child stopped and listened intently, as if trying to catch a whisper on the wind.

So they continued, past the outcrop of rocks, over the hill, and down the steep face. Suddenly the girl's small hand clutched the sleeve of the man's coat. A faint bleating swirled around on the wind.

"There, Father!" she cried and pointed to the hillside.

They fought their way against the wind to the rocky outcrop.

"Over there!"

They climbed down the slope together. A small lamb lay wedged between the rocks. Gently, the shepherd eased the lamb out and tucked it under his woollen gansey. Then with a smile that warmed the wild moor, he said, "Come on lassie, let's go home."

Meg was a lively child, with a bubbly laugh, and hair that shone like spangled gold in the sun. She was a child of the moors, and loved nothing better than to listen to her father whistling and singing as he strode over the hills. She skipped by his side, and he laughed as she jumped and twirled, and frisked and frolicked like one of his lambs.

As she grew, he taught her all he knew of the moors, and how to tend the sheep and care for the small caddie lambs.

In the evenings, they watched the mist roll in over the hills and hang low across the moors. Then they sat together by the fire; she baked their round bannocks on a girdle hung from the swey, while he read to her and told her such stories of long ago that her eyes grew round and large.

The Gift of Values

So the happy years slipped by. Long warm summer days, roaming the hills and the beautiful glens and listening to the music of the rushing rivers that wound over slates and stones. Then the wildness of the harsh, yet lovely winters, with long quiet nights in the glow of the fire and the gentle light of the cruisie lamp.

And the shepherd watched as his little Meg grew before his eyes, until she stood almost as tall as he, and her golden hair fell below her waist. She was no longer a child, but a young woman and fair to the eyes.

Then one evening Meg hung the kettle from the crook and the links, and then turned to look at her father.

"Father, I have something to tell you. Please don't be too sad."

He stopped rocking his chair and his keen blue eyes searched her face.

Meg swallowed hard, and then said, "I'm going to go to Edinburgh, Father, and try for a job in the city. I'll be leaving soon."

The shepherd stared in amazement at his daughter. For a moment he couldn't say anything. His voice was low when he finally spoke. "But why, Meg?" he asked. "How could you leave our highlands? The heather and the moors?"

"I don't know, Father," she said. "You know I love the highlands. I do! But I want to go. I need to go. Please don't make it harder for me."

That night, the shepherd went to bed early and prayed for a long time.

On a brisk, cold morning, they stood together at the train station and waited for the train to come in. Their breath made white clouds in the air as they stomped their feet and clapped their gloved hands.

Meg could hardly bear to look at her father. She felt she would drown in the great sadness in his eyes.

"Och, lassie, must you be going?" he asked again in a low voice.

Meg threw her arms around him and hugged him hard. "Oh, Father!" she cried. "I'm sorry to leave you! But I'll write to you every week, I promise!"

As the train pulled away from the station, Meg waved from the window until her arm ached.

Her father watched her into the distance, and felt as if his heart was breaking. "Watch over my little girl," he prayed. Then with a sigh, he turned and made for home.

Meg's letters came every Friday, just as she had promised, and they sparkled with life. The shepherd smiled as she recounted her adventures, and shared with him all the wonders of the city. He could almost hear her voice as she described her room, and the job she had found. And every day as he walked the lonely moors, he carried her in his heart.

Summer came, and then faded into autumn, and the days grew crisp and chill. Eagerly, the shepherd waited for Meg's letters, but they no longer reached him every week. And when they did arrive, they no longer made him smile inside. More and more they troubled him. Was Meg unhappy? Perhaps his girl was unwell?

Then one night, as the wind licked and howled around the thatched cottage, he thought he heard her voice, tossing and crying on the gale. Was she calling him? He put his face in his hands and began to pray.

That same night in Edinburgh, Meg dreamed she was running over her beloved moors, laughing free. The sun was setting over the blue-purple hills and bathed the heather in a soft golden light. She was bounding and leaping from rock to rock, like one of her father's lambs. Suddenly she stumbled and fell. She began slipping and sliding towards the edge of the steep rock face.

"Father!"

She saw him running towards her, calling her name, arms outstretched. But it was too late. She was falling, falling, falling...

Meg sat bolt upright in bed, her heart pounding, cheeks wet with tears. Her breath came in ragged gasps. She looked around the room. Cold and dismal, it stared back at her with empty eyes.

Meg slumped against the bed end. *Why did I ever leave? If only I could… no! I could never go home now. Never.*

She covered her face with her hands. "Oh, Father," she whispered. "I'm so ashamed."

The Gift of Values

The shepherd awoke early the next morning, before the mists had cleared. He ate some brose from a wooden bowl, and then packed some bread and crowdie into his bag. With a final glance around the room, he headed out the door. He was going to find his girl.

Over the hills he walked, mile after mile. Past the shimmering lochs, through the glens where birch, larch and alder trees grew close to the water's edge. Past masses of huge piled-up and tumbled about rocks. On and on he went, fording ice-cold streams, full of stones and as clear as glass, stopping only to rest a short while in the shelter of a sheep stell, or a deserted barn.

So the shepherd made his way to Edinburgh.

It was a bleak and foggy day when he finally set foot on the cobblestone streets of the city. The air smelt stale and dank, not at all like the clean open air of the hills. Dark, grey buildings crowded around him, and the hustle and noise assailed him. Where to begin? How could he ever find her amongst all these people?

Then something stirred inside him and he knew what to do. He cupped his hands around his mouth, and his shepherd's call rang out, clear and loud. People stopped in their tracks and stared at the sight. Children pointed and laughed. But again and again he called, always watching, searching, listening.

Day after day, the shepherd combed the streets of Edinburgh. On every corner his call rang out. Night by night, he walked the dark alleys, searching the shadows for Meg's face.

A week went by and then another. His heart longed for the open hills, the simple music of the wind on the moors. Slowly, the hope of ever finding his girl faded and gave way to a deep despair. He must return empty-handed, empty-hearted and alone to the moors, where Meg's laughter was but a bittersweet memory. And as the pain of his grief overflowed his heart, he let out a call so sad, the empty street echoed with the sound, and the very wind seemed to weep.

It was then Meg heard it. A call so sweet, it unlocked a thousand memories in her mind.

The room seemed to fill with the fragrance of heather, chasing away the thick clouds of smoke and the smell of liquor. She was a child again, and the apple of her father's eye. People watched, startled, as Meg leapt to her feet and ran across the room. Tears streamed down her face. Out the door and down the stairs she sped, fleet-footed and sure. And as she ran, the darkness in her soul seemed to shrink and retreat and hope flooded her heart. The heavy wooden door groaned as she threw it open and ran out onto the dark, lonely street.

Her eyes found him in the shadows, just turning away, his shoulders hunched in sadness.

"Father!" she cried.

He stopped still. Slowly, he turned around.

"Meg!"

She saw his soft eyes fill with joy and tears. He loved her. She knew it. She ran across the street towards him, and as she did, all her hurt and shame rolled away. She buried her face in the rough warmth of his coat, as he held her and gently stroked her hair. Then with a smile that lit up the smoggy street, he said, "Come on, lassie, let's go home!"

Think About It

- ❖ What were Meg and her father searching for on the moors?
- ❖ Why did Meg decide to leave?
- ❖ Why did she feel she could never go home?
- ❖ Do you think her father felt hurt or rejected by her actions? Did he have to forgive?
- ❖ What did her father do when he reached Edinburgh?
- ❖ How did he find her?

The Gift of Values

- ❖ What did Meg feel when she saw her father and realised he still loved her?
- ❖ How does this story illustrate the love God has for us?

Something To Do

- ❖ Read the parables of the lost sheep and the prodigal son in *Luke 15*. Then act them out. It doesn't matter how rough it is, or how many 'mistakes' the children make. The important thing is you have fun doing it. It's such a great way for them to really remember the story. Another idea is to make up a puppet show. When we did this, we never dreamed that one day we'd use it on outreach in the Fiji Islands. These two parables are such a powerful illustration of the great love and forgiveness God has for each one of His children.

- ❖ Parents, this point is especially for you. After you've read this story, there is a window of opportunity to speak into the life of your children. Tell them that no matter what happens in their life, they will always be welcome back home; that no matter what they do, you will never stop loving them. Remind them that God is their Father, and that He will forgive any sin if they come to Him in repentance. Perhaps some of you need to go out and search for a child who is 'lost.' I'll never forget the day a young girl approached me after a concert. She was dressed all in black leather, and had more facial piercings than I'd ever seen before. But as she came towards me, I saw she was crying. "Rose," she said, "that song you sang about the shepherd and his daughter - I wish my father had come looking for me!"

- ❖ Explain to your children that there are a lot of people in the world who will never find their way into a church. That's why Jesus told us to go out into the highways and byways. Many people are just longing for someone to care enough to go looking for them. They need to hear that God is a forgiving God, and that He sent His son Jesus into the world

Forgiveness

to seek and save us. Think of ways together that you and your children could reach out to people around you.

❖ Parents, don't forget to share with your children how they can give their hearts to the Lord. So often, we leave it to the Sunday School teachers or the pastor. There is no greater joy than praying with your own child and leading them to Jesus. A simple heart prayer is all you need.

Dear God,
I'm sorry for all the wrong things I've done. Please forgive me and make me your child. Thank you Jesus for dying on the cross for my sins. Come into my heart and show me how to live the way You want me to.
In Jesus' name, Amen.

❖ Listen to the song *Shepherd's Call* on our website: *www.boomfamily.co.nz*

❖ Do a research project together on the life of John Newton, the slave trader whose life was transformed by the power of forgiveness. Sing together his wonderful hymn, *Amazing Grace*.

Boom Clip

My father was crossing the Cook Strait on the ferry when he heard someone whistling a song. Immediately, the words of the old Sunday School song rushed into Dad's heart.

> *Wide, wide as the ocean*
> *High as the heavens above*
> *Deep, deep as the deepest sea*
> *Is my Saviour's love*
> *I though so unworthy*
> *Still am a child of His care*
> *For His word teaches me*
> *That His love reaches me*
> *Everywhere.*

Dad looked out at the vast blue sea all around him. And the revelation of the fullness and greatness of God's forgiveness flooded his heart. Right then, in the middle of the Cook Strait, Dad gave his heart back to the Lord.

Boom Clip

One morning in devotions, I asked the children how they would describe God. Jacob's hand shot up. "Magic!" he said. Everyone had a bit of a laugh. "You mean He can work miracles," said Josiah. Jacob nodded vigorously.

"I know," said Sam. "He's nice." More laughter.

"Kind's probably a better word," said one of the older ones. So, having heard my little ones describe God as 'nice' and 'magic', I decided we'd take a look at God's character. Over the next week, we talked about the character of God as described in *Exodus 34:5-7*, and memorised the passage.

"Then the Lord came down in the cloud and stood there with him [Moses] and proclaimed His name, the Lord. And He passed in front of Moses proclaiming, "The Lord, the Lord, the compassionate and gracious

God, slow to anger and abounding in love and faithfulness, maintaining love to thousands, and forgiving wickedness, rebellion and sin. Yet He does not leave the guilty unpunished."

Now when I ask the children what they think God's like, they come up with some really good answers!

So Said...

- "Never forget the three powerful resources you always have available to you: love, prayer and forgiveness." *H.Jackson Brown, Jr*

- "Forgiveness is a funny thing: it warms the heart and cools the sting." *William Arthur Ward*

- "I never forgive and I never forget," said *General Oglethorpe* to *John Wesley*. Wesley replied, "Then, Sir, I hope you never sin."

- "The goal of forgiveness is restoration and reconciliation of relationship." *Wendy Bray and Chris Ledger*

- "His heart was as great as the world, but there was no room in it to hold the memory of a wrong.' *Emerson* (said of Lincoln)

- "There is no love without forgiveness, and there is no forgiveness without love." *Bryant*

Words To Live By

- "If You, O Lord, kept a record of sins, O lord, who could stand? But with You there is forgiveness; therefore you are feared." *Psalm 130:3,4 NIV*

- "We are His people and the sheep of His pasture." *Psalm 100:3 NASB*

- "Like a shepherd he will tend His flock, in his arm he will gather the lambs, and carry them in his bosom; he will gently lead the nursing ewes." *Isaiah 40:11 NIV*

The Gift of Values

- "In him we have redemption through His blood, the forgiveness of sins, in accordance with the riches of God's grace that he lavished on us with all wisdom and understanding." *Ephesians 1:7,8 NIV*

- "He forgave all our sins, having cancelled the written code, with its regulations, that was against us and that stood opposed to us; he took it away, nailing it to the cross." *Colossians 2:13,14 NIV*

- "If we confess our sins, he is faithful and just and will forgive our sins and purify us from all unrighteousness." *1 John 1:9 NIV*

- "You have put all my sins behind Your back." *Isaiah 38:17 NIV*

- "He does not treat us as our sins deserve or repay us according to our iniquities. For as high as the heavens are above the earth, so great is His love for those who fear Him; as far as the east is from the west, so far has he removed our transgressions from us." *Psalm 103:10 - 12 NIV*

Dig Deeper

- Read *The Runaway's Revenge* by Dave and Neta Jackson. Young Hamilton Jones is bent on revenge. He tracks down the slave trader responsible for bringing his mother to the United States, determined to make him pay for all their suffering. But the man he meets is nothing like the horrible person he's imagined. John Newton is a changed man.

- Read with your younger children *The Runaway Son* in the *Ready to Read Series* by Nick and Claire Page.

- Read *Back to School* by Wanda Brunstetter. Rachel Yoder, a young Amish girl, learns life lessons about love and forgiveness.

ಅ

The Colour Of Spring

She had lived all her life in the same house with her parents, sister and aunt. For forty-eight years her life had been as regular as clockwork, as stable as the huge grandfather clock that had stood for eighty years in the hall.

Then, in May 1940, she and her family were sucked into the maelstrom of war. It's hard to imagine how her ordinary life could undergo such a huge transformation in just a few short months. The middle-aged spinster became an underground worker, saving the lives of many Jews. Her name was Corrie ten Boom.

Then on February 28, 1944, everything she knew was taken from her. Corrie, Betsie and their beloved father were arrested. His last words as the guards led him away were, "God goes with you, my daughters!" They never saw him again. Corrie and Betsie were taken to Ravensbruck, a Nazi concentration camp. Sorrow, hardship and tears became their daily bread.

But one night, Betsie had a dream. Excitedly she told Corrie about it.

"Corrie, we are going to get out of here! And when we do, we must travel the world and tell people that it doesn't matter how deep the pit is, God's love is deeper still." Her blue eyes sparkled. "They will believe us, Corrie, because we have been here!"

Corrie was miraculously released some months later through a clerical error and, true to Betsie's dream, she spent the rest of her life travelling the world, visiting over sixty countries with a powerful message.

"There is no pit so deep, but that God's love is deeper still."

And people believed her, because she had proved it to be true in a Nazi concentration camp.

The pale, gaunt faces gazed hungrily at Corrie ten Boom as she shared with them about God's love. "Anger and bitterness will keep you prisoners even though the war is over," she told them. "Only forgiveness and God's love can set you completely free." She smiled at her audience as she held up her worn Bible.

The Gift of Values

"Freely you have received, freely give. Has not Christ forgiven you? Ja, ja! So too, you must forgive everyone who has hurt you," she urged. "Not just the guards who beat you, but also your fellow Dutchmen, the ones who turned you in. Perhaps that is the hardest thing to forgive, ne?"

Corrie knew that only too well. She remembered how hard it had been for her to write the letter to the man who had betrayed her family to the Germans. It was one of the most difficult things she had ever done. But oh, the joy she felt once she had penned her forgiveness!

Everywhere Corrie went, her message was the same. If she closed her eyes, she could still see the glow on Betsie's face as she shared her dream.

In time, Corrie discovered that some of the people who most needed to hear the wonderful message of forgiveness were those she met in Germany. Germany was a land in ruin; cities of ashes and rubble. Nine million people were homeless. But more painful still, the hearts and minds of the people lay in ruins.

One day, Corrie gazed out over a church congregation in Munich. She had just shared her heart with them. Had they heard? Did they understand that God is the God who forgives? She watched and prayed as they slowly and quietly filed out of the church.

Then she saw him. He held a brown felt hat in his hands and was coming straight towards her. It was the former S.S. officer who had stood guard at the shower room in Ravensbruck. Time stood still. The church faded away and suddenly it was all there again - the roomful of mocking men, the heaps of clothing, the feeling of shame, and Betsie's pain-blanched face. Corrie felt as if she could scarcely breathe.

The guard came towards her, beaming. "Thank you, Fraulein, for your message! How wonderful it is to know that God has washed away my sins!" He held out his hand.

Corrie stood there, frozen, her arm by her side. Angry, vengeful thoughts boiled inside her. She tried not to think of Betsie wincing beneath his cruel blows. Even as the angry thoughts stormed inside her, Corrie saw the sin of them. *Dear God, forgive me for these thoughts and help me to forgive him.*

She tried to smile, tried to raise her hand. She couldn't. She felt nothing, not even one small spark of warmth or charity. She breathed another silent prayer. *Jesus, I cannot forgive him. Give me Your forgiveness.* Then she reached out and took his hand. And as she did, a current of warmth seemed to shoot through her arm and hand, and into his. Love and forgiveness filled her heart. She lifted her eyes and smiled at her former captor. She was truly free.

Sometime later, Corrie was approached by the director of a relief agency in Germany. "Corrie, we have such a need for rehabilitation work here in Germany. Please will you help us? We have found just the place!"

Together they drove to Darmstadt. Corrie climbed out of the car and stared at the former concentration camp. Rolls of rusting barbed wire still surrounded it. She walked slowly up the cinder path between the drab grey barracks. The door creaked as she pushed it open. Inside, were rows of metal cots.

She stared at them in silence as painful memories flooded into her mind. Then she turned and said, "Window boxes. We'll have them at every window. The barbed wire must come down, of course, and we'll need lots of paint. Green paint. Bright yellow-green. The colour of things coming up new in the spring!"

Think About It

❖ Do you think Corrie found it easy to forgive?

❖ Do we have to wait for the feelings of forgiveness before we forgive?

❖ Discuss Corrie's comment that you can still be a prisoner even after you have been physically released from prison.

The Gift of Values

- ❖ What did Corrie say could keep a person as a prisoner?
- ❖ How did Corrie manage to forgive the former guard?
- ❖ What does the word rehabilitation mean?
- ❖ Why did Corrie choose to paint the former concentration camp in the colours of spring? (Forgiveness is like spring. It births new hope, joy and peace in our lives. Life is filled with promise again. We can start over again.)
- ❖ When we choose *not* to forgive, what are some of the outcomes?
- ❖ Why did Jesus tell us to 'love our enemies and pray for those who persecute us?' (*Matthew 5:44*) As we pray for our enemies, the power of forgiveness is released in our own lives.

Something To Do

- ❖ Do a research project on the life of Corrie ten Boom.
- ❖ Paint a picture of spring. Use the same colours that Corrie chose. You could paint a garden and have the blessings of forgiveness growing like flowers.
- ❖ Think together of ways you can apologise to people. Write them down on a blackboard. Here are some we thought of: saying sorry with words; writing a note or letter; making a phone call; making restitution (discuss what this means; giving a hug).
- ❖ Get the children to demonstrate some of the different ways you can say, "Sorry" - both genuine apologies and insincere ones. We had a hilarious time doing this. One of Jacob's examples was, "Sooorry!"- said with a shake of the head, a roll of the eyes and promptly followed by a sticking out of the tongue! The children all knew exactly which ones were sincere, and which were totally deficient. It really helped them to understand the

truth that an apology must come from the heart, and also how easy it is to spot a fake apology.

❖ Discuss the verse in Ephesians that says, 'Do not let the sun go down while you are still angry, and do not give the devil an opportunity." *Ephesians 4:26,27 NIV*

❖ Get each child to paint a sunset, and then write the above verse across the bottom. Pin it by their bed as a reminder.

❖ Read the story of Joseph and his brothers in *Genesis, Chapters 42-45*.

Boom Clip

I will never forget the day I saw first-hand the pain of unforgiveness. Mrs. Brown had come into the doctor's medical practice where I worked as a nurse. As I took her blood pressure, she poured out her heart to me. "I can't sleep, I can't eat. Every time I close my eyes, I see my boy lying on the hospital bed, mangled and broken." She began to cry. "I feel as if I'm being eaten up on the inside."

I released the air from the sphygmometer. Her blood pressure was dangerously high. I put my hand on hers.

"He gets out today!" she sobbed. "The boy that killed my son. Five miserable years. That's all he got. He should be in prison for life."

Mrs. Brown's son had been sitting on his motorbike on the side of the road, talking to a friend, when a drunken driver had slammed into the back of him at a hundred kilometres an hour. Ben suffered terrible injuries as he was catapulted fifty metres along the tar seal. He was unrecognizable when his mother saw him at the hospital. He died shortly after.

The drunken driver was a young boy, just seventeen years old. He had been devastated by what had happened. His life would never be the same. I looked at Mrs Brown. Her marriage was in difficulty. Her health was failing. She was an absolute mess.

The Gift of Values

"I can't forgive him!" she cried, looking at me with anguished eyes. "I can never forgive him for what he did to my boy - to me!"

It was amazing. She already knew instinctively what she needed to do, if she was ever to survive this tragedy. I saw the deep pain in her eyes as she talked with me, and prayed for the words to share with her about the power of forgiveness.

So Said...

❖ "To forgive is to set a prisoner free and discover the prisoner was you." *Lewis B. Smedes*

❖ "When a deep injury is done, we never recover until we forgive." *Alan Paton*

❖ "In our relationships, let us aim to always be the first to bury the hatchet." *R.J Boom*

❖ "Up in the church tower is a bell which is rung by pulling on a rope. After the sexton lets go of the rope, the bell keeps swinging. First ding, then dong. Slower and slower until there's a final dong and it stops. When we forgive someone, we take our hands off the rope. But if we've been tugging at our grievances for a long time, we shouldn't be surprised when the old angry thoughts keep coming for a while. They're just the ding-dongs of the old bell slowing down." *Corrie Ten Boom*

❖ "You will always be a victim until you forgive. When you truly forgive, you open the channels through which trust and unconditional love can flow. One of the greatest deposits you can make in your relationships with other family members - and in the basic quality and richness of your own life - is to forgive." *Steven R. Covey*

❖ "Forgiveness is not an emotion, it's a decision." *Randall Worley*

- "Never does the human soul appear so strong as when it foregoes revenge, and dares forgive an injury." *E. H. Chapin*

- "Forgiveness is me giving up my right to hurt you for hurting me." *Anon*

- "To forgive is the highest, most beautiful form of love. In return, you will receive untold peace and happiness." *Robert Muller*

- "The man who forgives pays a tremendous price - the price of the evil he forgives! If I break a priceless heirloom that you treasure and you forgive me, you bear the loss and I go free." *David Augsberger*

- "Forgiveness is the fragrance the violet sheds on the heel that has crushed it." *Mark Twain*

Boom Clip

Angel, our Jack Russell terrier barked excitedly at the bottom of a totara tree. A large possum sat high in the branches. Chris went back to the barn to get his gun, while Angel kept the possum bailed up the tree. (Possums do immeasurable damage to the native trees in New Zealand and are considered a real pest.) When the gun dropped the possum into the river below, Angel leaped in after it. It was bigger than she was! She grabbed it and began swimming for the bank. But she couldn't drag it out no matter how hard she tried. We watched as she swam around and around with her prize, sinking lower and lower in the water until only her nose was above the surface.

"Let it go!" we shouted, but there was no way she was going to let it go, even if she drowned in the process! Silly dog. We couldn't stop laughing. Finally Josiah reached down and rescued her.

It was a real lesson to me. How often do we hang on to things, even when they are destroying us? Worry, wrong relationships, unforgiveness. We need to let them go.

The Gift of Values

Words To Live By

- "Love keeps no record of wrongs." *1 Corinthians 13:5 NIV*

- "Forgive, and you will be forgiven." *Luke 6:37 NIV* (The Greek word here means 'to fully release, dismiss, pardon, let go, loose, set at liberty.')

- "Forgive us our sins, for we also forgive everyone who sins against us." *Luke 11:4 NIV*

- "For if you forgive men when they sin against you, your heavenly Father will also forgive you. But if you do not forgive men their sins, your Father will not forgive your sins." *Matthew 6:14, 15 NIV*

Dig Deeper

- There are many great books to read about the life of Corrie ten Boom. Some we have enjoyed are: *A Prisoner and Yet* by Corrie ten Boom; *Corrie ten Boom; Heroine of Haarlem* by Sam Wellman; *The Hiding Place* by John and Elizabeth Sherrill. (This has also been released as a movie, suitable for older children.)

- Read the book, *Lorna Doone* by Richard D. Blackmore, or watch the DVD. It demonstrates the destructive power of unforgiveness and family feuds.

- Watch *Little Women* together. A great family movie. Amy burns Jo's book - an unpardonable offence to her sister! Jo refuses to forgive Amy, and things are only resolved after a near-fatal drama on the ice.

- Read *A Spark Neglected Burns the House* by Leo Tolstoy. When a quarrel breaks out between neighbours over the simple matter of an egg, an entire village suffers the consequences of unforgiveness. Another brilliant short story by Tolstoy.

Epilogue

Last night Chris and I sat together on our porch swing and drank in the beauty of the still night. All the children were asleep inside the barn, and a full moon shone on the fields. What a beautiful sight. I will always remember it as the night I finished writing *The Gift of Values - Volume Two*. What a wonderful journey it has been. My own spirit has been built up and encouraged as I've searched the Scriptures, read inspirational material and recorded some of the 'happenings' in the Boom family. I can't wait to begin writing Volume Three!

The Gift of Values - Volume Three will cover the following values:

Friendship
Humility
Joy
Faithfulness
Kindness
Integrity

If you would like to receive notification of when Volume Three is published, please email me at *thegiftofvalues@rosieboom.com* and simply write *The Gift of Values - Volume Three* in the subject line, and I will contact you as soon as it is available.

When I was in Colorado this year, I heard a song about the boy who offered his small lunch of fish and bread to Jesus. As I listened, I realised that this book is like the little boy's lunch - small and insignificant maybe, but the Lord can bless it and multiply it to feed and bless many people. I offer it to Him and hope and pray it will be a blessing to many families.

Rosie

Acknowledgments

Thank you: **Mum** and **Dad**, for your amazing commitment in helping me write this book. Thank you for teaching the children each Wednesday so I could find some uninterrupted time to write. You truly are amazing.

Altus, for yet another story from your childhood! I can just see you sitting under a tree with chicken dung plastered on your lip and a grim look of determination on your face. I wish I'd known you back then - we would have had a few laughs!

Penelope, for your enthusiasm and belief in what I'm doing. You're the best sister anyone could have.

HSM Publishing, for making this book accessible to families around the world.

Joseph, for your wonderful help in editing. I can't wait to read your book.

Josiah, Kate, Eliza, Milly, Samuel and **Jacob** - what would this book be without you? Thanks for letting me use all your little stories and Boom clips. Thank you for doing all the extra work around the barn so Mum could sit and write! And thank you for filling my life with so much joy.

Chris, my best friend, and the love of my life for the past twenty years. Thank you for being so patient with your 'Mrs Tappity Tap Tap'! I know how much you've had to pick up the slack while I've been writing, and yet you always do it so cheerfully. What a year it's been, living together in the barn! God has been good to us.

More from the Boom family album

Hopefully you'll be able to catch a glimpse of our life in the barn with these photos! The children are growing so fast, just like the young oaks we've planted on our land.

Every day seems to be packed full of fun, work, challenges, laughter and… I have to say, dirt and mud.

Working hard on the land.

Milly

Eliza

Samuel

The Gift of Values

The Barn

Josiah

Kate

Jacob exploring the river.

Milly, Jacob and Samuel enjoying the mud!

Chris and Rosie… twenty years on.

About the Author

Rosie lives with her husband, Chris, and their six children, Josiah (19), Kate (18), Eliza (15), Emily (12), Samuel (10) and Jacob (8) in Whangarei, New Zealand.

Rosie spent three years as a young child in Papua New Guinea, where her parents were missionaries. After graduating from her nursing training, she spent a year in Borneo as a missionary. It was here that Chris came to visit her and declare his love - the rest is history!

Rosie and Chris are singer/songwriters, and have had the joy of encouraging and challenging Christians in many different countries. They have released a number of CDs which are available on their web site. Rosie has also published a children's book, *The Happy Prince*.

Rosie is a sought after speaker at women's conferences, missions and home-schooling conventions, and churches, where she loves to speak about her passions - missions, family, and Jesus.

For speaking engagements and bookings, contact Rosie at:

Boom Tree Publishing
Rosie Boom
549 Kara Rd, R.D. 9 Whangarei, New Zealand
Email: *rosie@rosieboom.com*
Rosie's Blog: *www.rosieboom.com*
Website: *www.rosieboom.com*

Other books by Rosie Boom

The Barn Chronicles: Books 1–4

Where Lions Roar at Night

This book is the first in *The Barn Chronicles* series, and tells of the exciting, humorous adventures of the Boom family as they make their home in a 90-year-old barn. They are suitable for primary age readers, or to be read to children by parents.

Winner of the 2010 CALEB PRIZE for Best Children's Book

Where Arrows Fly

Where Arrows Fly is the sequel to *Where Lions Roar at Night* and is the second book in The Barn Chronicles series. Read about the continuing adventures of the Boom family and the everyday joys and challenges of the 'simple life'.

Winner of the 2011 CALEB PRIZE for Best Children's Book

Where the Crickets Sing

Where the Crickets Sing, the third book in *The Barn Chronicles* series, invites the reader to join the Boom family in another year of homesteading in rural New Zealand.

Finalist in the 2012 CALEB PRIZE for Best Children's Book
Winner 2013 Christian Small Publishers International Book of the Year Award Children's Category

Where the River Rises

As the Boom family begins a fourth year of living in their 93-year-old barn, a terrible drought has Northland in its grip. The time has finally come to leave the barn and begin a whole new adventure...

2013 CSP Book of the YearAward - Best Children's Book

Where the Jungle Calls

A long time before The Barn Chronicles, Rose lived in the big city. But one day her life changed forever ...

Rose, Penny and Peter find themselves swept away into a great adventure, sailing the blue Pacific to a mission school deep in the jungles of Papua. There they become adventurers and explorers in their own wild kingdom. But there are hidden dangers lurking: snakes, scorpions, jerry-wars, malaria – and in the sea and rivers fearsome crocodiles ...

Here in the jungles of New Guinea the readers of *The Barn Chronicles* will meet their favourite characters again in a different time, a different place. This is where their adventures first began.

www.ingramcontent.com/pod-product-compliance
Lightning Source LLC
Chambersburg PA
CBHW061939220426
43662CB00012B/1968